The Quixtar Price Is Right!

INTI
PUBLISHING

The Quixtar Price Is Right

by Dr. Bill Quain

Copyright 2003 by Bill Quain and Steve Price

Printed in United States of America
First edition June 2003

ISBN: 1-891279-12-2

Published by INTI Publishing
intipublishing.com
Tampa, FL

Cover design and text layout by Parry Design Studio

Dedication

This book is dedicated to my grandfathers, Hugh Haggerty and John Ryan. Both men were successful business owners and entrepreneurs. They taught me business principles with humor, with stories, and by setting good examples. I hope I can do the same for you.

Acknowledgments

The acronym *TEAM* stands for *"Together Everyone Achieves More."* Truer words were never written—especially when your teammates are Katherine Glover and Dr. Steve Price of INTI Publishing.

Whether it's creating new ideas... helping with painstaking rewrites... designing covers and layouts... or marketing, Steve and Katherine do it with style—and with a smile! Thanks, guys. You're the best!

What You Will Learn from This Book

*Whenever you see a successful business,
rest assured that someone once made a
courageous decision.*

—Peter Drucker
management guru

I'm a college teacher. And teachers, as you know, love to give pop quizzes. See if you can solve this brain teaser:

What costs 39 cents on Monday, 79 cents on Tuesday, and $2.50 on Wednesday?

Give up?

The answer is a 3-ounce bag of popcorn!

Huh? How can the price of a tiny bag of popcorn increase to more than six times its original price in only two days? Simple. Follow along as I tell you the story of the popping prices of the popping corn.

Prices Are Like Unplanned Vacations—All Over the Map!

For the last five years, our family has taken a month-long vacation in the Northeast. Before leaving on our most recent vacation, we stopped at the local supermarket to stock up on groceries. One of the items we bought was a six-pack of 3-ounce bags of microwave popcorn for $2.36, which calculates to 39 cents per 3-ounce bag.

Within two days my extended family had devoured the six-pack of popcorn, so we walked across the street to a convenience store and bought several 3-ounce bags for 79 cents each.

The next morning a day-long rain set in. So, we gathered up the clan and headed to the movies. Can't see a movie without popcorn, right? I bought each of our two girls a small bag of popcorn. Cost per bag? $2.50.

Americans are expert consumers, but very few Americans are expert business owners.

So, there you have it. I bought the same product on three different days in three different businesses, and I paid three different prices ranging from a low of 39 cents... to a high *of $2.50—an increase of more than 500%!*

Now, as a consumer, you may be thinking, *"How can 'Business A' get away with pricing a product six times higher than 'Business B,' located just two blocks down the street?"*

And, as an independent business owner, you may be asking, *"How do businesses set their product prices, and what is the correlation between prices and profits?"*

These are great questions. This book will not only answer these questions, but will also give you scores of powerful insights into the business side of the buyer/seller transaction.

Experts in Consuming, but Amateurs in Business

If you stop to think about it, *Americans are expert consumers.* (Little wonder, considering how often we buy goods and services and how inundated we are with advertisements and commercials). *But very few Americans are expert business owners.* Why? Because we're taught from an early age to think like consumers, instead of business owners.

From the time we can walk, we're taught to reach across the store counter and hand cash or credit cards to the cashier in exchange for goods or services. But very few of us have been taught to appreciate and understand the business owner's side of the store counter. As a result, most people don't understand how prices are set and how profits are made. As a consumer, you don't have to know these things. But as a business owner, you MUST understand the relationship between pricing and profits or you won't be in business for long!

Think of this book as a crash course in independent business ownership. I'm going to take you by your consumer hand, lead you around to the other side of the counter, and then teach you the key business principles that every business owner needs to understand in order to operate a profitable enterprise.

Why Me? Why Quixtar?

I feel especially qualified to offer advice on business in general—as well as Quixtar in particular—because of my background as a business owner, college professor, consultant, author, and speaker.

First of all, I've had a life-long love affair with business. My parents were small business owners, so I grew up in a household where the talk at the dinner table centered around owner-type issues, as opposed to employee-type issues. The dinner lessons must have taken, for, at age 19, I owned a hotel and a restaurant.

> **When I hear some IBOs and prospects talk about lowering prices, I know they haven't made the mental leap from thinking like a consumer to thinking like a business owner.**

For the last 25 years, I've taught business and marketing courses at four different colleges. When I'm not in the classroom, I consult with companies, write books, and speak. My consulting specialty is helping companies make more money, and my business-consulting book, *10 Places Where Money Is Hidden in Your Business—and How to Find It,* is in its 10th printing. I've spoken to dozens of traditional corporations, including Coca-Cola and the Hyatt Corporation. In addition, since the publication of my bestselling book, *Pro-sumer Power,* I've had the privilege of speaking to tens of thousands of Quixtar IBOs in dozens of cities across the country.

Given my varied business experience over the last 30 years and given my person-to-person interaction with Quixtar IBOs during the last five years, I think I'm uniquely positioned to offer some practical business insights that will help IBOs get the most out of Quixtar's non-traditional, yet incredibly dynamic, business model.

Right Idea, Wrong Solution

During my many conversations with IBOs, I've learned that the vast majority of new IBOs have backgrounds as employees, and, thus, lack basic knowledge as to what it takes to own and operate a successful business. For example, one of the most common questions I hear from new IBOs and their prospects is, "Why doesn't Quixtar become a discount buying club and then everyone will want to buy from them?" The second most frequent comment I get is, "I don't want to make money from my friends."

What astounds me isn't the frequency of these two comments, but the depth of misunderstanding about the nature of business ownership that would lead someone to concern themselves with these issues. Then it suddenly hit me—IBOs who make comments like these are looking at The Business from a *consumer's point of view,* as opposed to a *business person's point of view.* Consumers are discount driven, so they evaluate their performance accordingly: *"How do I shop so as to buy more stuff for less money?"*

Business owners, on the other hand, are profit driven, so they evaluate their performance just the opposite of consumers: *"How do I market so as to sell more stuff for higher prices?"*

So, when I hear some IBOs and prospects talk about *lowering* prices, I know they haven't made the mental leap from thinking like a consumer to thinking like a business owner. Yes, everyone in The Business would agree that *increasing profits is the right idea.* But as a consultant to dozens of businesses, I can tell you flat out that *lowering prices is the wrong way to go about it!*

It's Smarter to Add Value Than to Lower Prices

My consulting specialty is helping hotels and restaurants make more money. When I meet with owners and managers, they ask me business-related questions, such as: How do we add value? How do we improve service? How do we attract more customers? No client, however, has ever called me and said, "I need you to come over and help me lower my prices." Why? Because successful business owners understand that it's smarter to add value than to lower prices.

Consumers have become increasingly obsessed with buying at the lowest prices.

Sure, lowering prices is one of dozens of marketing strategies available to business owners. Nothing like a clearance sale to clear the shelves for new merchandise. But more often than not, business owners want to know how to *increase prices* and increase traffic, so that they can make even bigger profits.

Consumers, on the other hand, have become increasingly obsessed with buying at the lowest prices. They brag about the "great deals" they get at Sam's Club, and chide friends and acquaintances who pay a buck or two more than they paid for a jumbo box of detergent.

But the simple truth is, prices have always been relative. For example, the price of gas at the local marina where I fill up my boat is nearly double the price at the gas station down the street. Common sense would tell you to buy the gas for your boat at the gas station instead and carry it out to the boat. But if you've ever lugged 10, five-gallon tanks 200 yards to fill up a boat, you'll readily agree that the convenience of pulling up to a marina is well worth the extra money, proving that intangibles are a big part of every business's pricing strategies.

The Best Fruit May Require a Bit More Effort

A word of caution: In order for you to fully understand how pricing impacts your business, I've found it necessary to include some background information about the different kinds of business models. As you're aware, Quixtar has a unique business model, and by comparing Quixtar with more traditional models, you will gain a better understanding as to why The Business is unequalled when one compares the ridiculously low cost of entry to the upside profit potential.

Also, because parts of the book are rich in business concepts, you may need to read some of the chapters several times in order to fully grasp the material. Trust me when I tell you that the extra time and effort will be well worth it.

So, without further delay, let's turn the page and get started learning how to maximize the Quixtar opportunity by thinking and acting like *independent business owners...* instead of *dependent business consumers.*

Also by Bill Quain, PhD

- *Reclaiming the American Dream*

- *10 Rules to Break & 10 Rules to Make*

- *Pro-sumer Power!*

- *B2B Means "Back to Basics"*

Table of Contents

1 "Come on Down!" 1

2 Don't Get Caught Napping on the 9
Consumer Couch!

3 Understand and Honor Your Business Model 15

4 How Prices Are Set 25

5 How Quixtar Prices Are Set 39

6 Market the Monsters! 55

7 Home Ownership: Business-Think 63
in Action

8 Consumer Discounts vs. Business Discounts 73

9 Pro-sumer Plus 79

10 The Purpose of Business 101

Come on Down!

Today, the future occupation of all
children is to be skilled consumers.

—David Riesman (1950)

Ah-h-h!

You're on vacation. You have a weekday morning all to yourself—such a rare luxury! You pour yourself a cup of coffee, click on the TV, and settle into your favorite chair with the morning newspaper.

Suddenly, you're startled by wild cheering exploding from your TV set. You glance up from your newspaper to see a hoard of screaming middle-aged men and women wildly waving their arms at you. Then you hear the announcer's unmistakable baritone voice.

"Melinda Johnson, COME ON DOWN!"

The crowd roars its approval.

"Tom Madden, COME ON DOWN!"

The second roar drowns out the first.

"Brenda Cherry, COME ON DOWN!"

The wave of screams builds as the first four audience members are directed to "come on down." You watch as the camera tracks to a safe perch above the stage, revealing a wide-angle view of two blue-haired women and two chubby middle-aged men sprinting madly down the aisle to the front stage.

Welcome to yet another episode of *The Price Is Right,* hosted by TV legend Bob Barker.

The Perfect Consumer TV Show

You watch spellbound as silver-haired Bob Barker, imperially trim and Hollywood tanned, banters with the guests. He seamlessly guides the talk to the first challenge of today's show, guessing the price of a children's outdoor playground set. The contestant whose guess is closest to the retail price without going over is the winner. The audience screams advice at the jittery contestants.

"$631," giggles contestant number one.

"$1,450," stutters contestant number two.

"$1,100," gushes contestant number three.

"$1,451," blurts contestant number four.

"The actual retail price is $2,470," Bob Barker croons through a bright-white smile. The audience roars its approval. The winner raises her arms and squeals with delight as razzle-dazzle music blares in the background.

The audience "oohs" and "aahs" with envy as veteran announcer Rod Roddy describes the "incredible prizes"—everything from bars of soap to barbells to brand new cars, lovingly eulogized in carefully crafted 10-second sound bites.

Five days a week the show gives away a truck-load of stuff to average people, just like you and me (40,000 contestants have appeared on *The Price Is Right* over the years). Unlike the long-running daytime game show *Jeopardy,* the contestants on *The Price Is Right* don't need to be smart. Or well read. They just have to guess product prices, a skill that every single American has mastered during countless hours of mall crawling and window shopping. Little wonder that *The Price Is Right* is the oldest and highest rated daytime game show on TV.

Ever Wonder What Happens on the Other Side of the TV Screen?

What makes *The Price Is Right* so popular? Simple—*the program is a one-hour valentine to consumerism!* Each episode offers dozens of products (if you don't like this one, wait 10 seconds and another product is on the way). Every consumer finds something to like about *The Price Is Right*. It's fast-paced. It's fun. And every second of every one-hour episode is designed to titillate our inner consumer. Yep, *The Price Is Right* is a Cupid's arrow of consumerism aimed right at our covetous hearts, and Bob Barker is the unerring archer.

> **The TV show "The Price Is Right" is a one-hour valentine to consumerism!**

But have you ever watched *The Price Is Right* and wondered what was happening on the other side of the TV screen—the business side? Be honest—do you think *The Price Is Right* would have lasted 30 years if the producers and network executives had the same fun-and-games attitude as the viewers? What if the vice presidents of CBS played silly pricing games all day long?... jumped up and down and giggled every time Bob Barker made a joke?... wore goofy hats and took tours of CBS studios after each show was over? Truth is, if the people on the business side of *The Price Is Right* had acted like the contestants and the viewers at home, the program wouldn't have lasted 30 minutes on CBS, much less 30 years, wouldn't you agree?

Show Business: PART Show... but ALL Business

The Price Is Right continues to be the Energizer Bunny of daytime TV programming for one reason and one reason only—the program is great for business.

> **"Show business" is PART show... but ALL business.**

In a word, the program makes CBS money. *Buckets and buckets of money!*

The Price Is Right has been a top daytime money producer for CBS for more than three decades. No wonder CBS changed the name of Stage 33 in CBS Television City to Bob Barker Studio—*he's made the network hundreds of millions over the years!*

Which is why I say "show business" is PART show... but ALL business. The *show* part of show business is the art of knowing which emotional buttons to push to create loyal viewers. The *business* part is the science of building a profitable business model and then duplicating the profitable processes over and over again. Obviously, CBS and the producers of *The Price Is Right* have mastered both the art and the science of show business.

Make It Your Business to Understand Your Business

In other words, successful business owners think and act like business owners, not consumers. That's why I say successful business owners make it their business to understand their business. Yes, part of understanding your business means understanding consumers. *But successful business owners rely on business strategies, as opposed to consumer strategies, to produce profits and grow their enterprises.*

On the other hand, the contestants on *The Price Is Right* use consumer strategies to guess the prices of the products featured on the show. The contestants use their experiences as shoppers to guess the prices of products, which is why their guesses are all over the board. Because the contestants don't have to manufacture and market the products, they're clueless about how prices are really set.

Successful business owners think and act like business owners, not consumers.

But you'd better believe that successful business owners understand pricing. Business owners don't just randomly pick prices for their products out of thin air, like some of the contestants on *The Price Is Right.* Successful business owners factor in dozens of variables and then set fair and reasonable prices that offer consumers a good value while creating a profit for the owner.

Because so many IBOs are employees with very little business experience, they try to evaluate The Business by applying their experiences as consumers. Consumers are conditioned to believe that "cheaper is better," so it's no surprise that many prospects and new IBOs mistakenly try to apply the "cheaper is better" philosophy to evaluating the Quixtar product line. Big mistake. To be successful, people need to take off their consumer hats and put on their business owner hats. Truth is, if you want what successful businesspeople have—that is, financial freedom... security... a great lifestyle... a college fund for your kids, etc.—then you have to *do* what successful businesspeople do. And what successful businesspeople do is *make it their business to understand their business...* and then work at their business on a daily basis.

Successful business owners factor in dozens of variables and then set fair and reasonable prices that offer consumers a good value while creating a profit for the owner.

What You Will Learn in the Coming Chapters

In the coming chapters, I'm going to teach you about business from the business owner's perspective. You're going to learn how business works in general—and how your Quixtar business works in particular—so that you can get the most out of your business opportunity. Here are just a few of the business concepts that you're going to learn in the next 100 or so pages:

- How prices are set
- Why it's perfectly acceptable for different businesses to charge different prices for identical products
- What kind of business models are available and why it can be dangerous to mix models
- What advantages the Quixtar model has over traditional business models
- What the difference is between consumer discounts and business discounts
- Which Quixtar products produce the most profits
- What it means to be a "pro-sumer plus"
- How you can *do good* (for others) while *doing well* (for yourself)

When you chose to become a Quixtar independent business owner, you chose to become the owner of one of the most powerful, wealth-generating vehicles in history. This vehicle is fast, durable, and powerful. But to get the maximum performance out of your vehicle, you have to learn how to drive it and maintain it!

So, ladies and gentlemen, start your engines—and let's get rolling on the road to success!

Don't Get Caught Napping on the Consumer Couch!

Ownership, independence, and access to wealth should not be the privilege of a few. They should be the hope of every American.

—Paul O'Neill
U.S. Treasury Secretary

In the last chapter, I took you through the TV screen so that you could see what happens on the business side of *The Price Is Right*. Why? Because the vast majority of Americans have never been exposed to the inner workings of business.

As a business professor, I can tell you that when my students enter my classes, they're universally clueless about basic business ownership principles... *and I teach in the business department!* They don't know the first thing about how to grow a profitable business. *But as consumers—well, they're all valedictorians!*

Yep—thanks to our Consumer Culture, when it comes to spending money, Americans are experts. But we're members

9

of the Clueless Culture when it comes to business moxie. Let's see—we're experts when it comes to spending money... but clueless when it comes to making money. How did that happen?

Blame it on the Consumer Couch.

The Consumer Couch—what's that all about? Follow along as I explain why we must fight the temptation to fall asleep on the Consumer Couch.

The Consumer Couch

If you're like most people, you have a nice, comfy couch in your TV room. This is the couch your family sits on, munching popcorn while watching your favorite sitcoms and made-for-TV movies.

This is the Consumer Couch. It's oh, so comfortable. Oh, so inviting. And, oh, so dangerous! *Dangerous? Did you say dangerous?* Where did that come from? The danger of the Consumer Couch is that it's so comfortable that we lie back and accept messages from the media at face value. Warmed by a blanket of newspaper and magazine ads and enraptured by the flickering firelight of the TV screen, we lie back on our Consumer Couch, lulled to sleep by a siren's voice that sings to us day and night, month after month, year after year. Over time, consumers hear certain messages so routinely that they begin to accept them as irrefutable fact:

> *"Buy on sale and 'save.'"*

> *"Deep discount stores are the best places to 'save' money."*

> **The danger of the Consumer Couch is that it's so comfortable that we lie back and accept messages from the media at face value.**

"The lower the prices, the better the store."

"The bigger the store, the better the shopping."

So, most Americans, having learned their lessons well, perform their duty as good little soldiers of commerce. They jump into their cars and drive to This-Mart and That-Mart, convinced that they're 'saving' $100 when they buy a $200 product at 50% off (when in reality, the only way to literally save $100 is to put it into a savings account and NOT spend it)!

But what really happens to consumers who try to "save" by buying cheaper is that they consume themselves into the poorhouse! The facts tell the tale: More Americans declare bankruptcy each year than graduate from college. More shopping centers are built than high schools. More people visit shopping malls than attend church.

Now are you beginning to see why I say, "Don't get caught napping on the Consumer Couch?" Get caught napping and you could wake up broke—financially and spiritually!

But what really happens to consumers who try to "save" by buying cheaper is that they consume themselves into the poorhouse! More Americans declare bankruptcy each year than graduate from college. More shopping centers are built than high schools. More people visit shopping malls than attend church.

Consumer Couch Potatoes

Don't get me wrong—I'm not saying that all consumerism is bad. Consuming is necessary. People exchanging money for goods and services is the backbone of a healthy economy. But today, all too many people have become Consumer Couch Potatoes. They only look at the world from one point of view—*the consumer's!*

> **Countless hours on the Consumer Couch have conditioned us to spend wealth, not create wealth.**

Consumer Couch Potatoes lie on their couch thinking about how comfortable it is... but they never think about the business that manufactured the couch. Consumer Couch Potatoes watch their TV sets religiously... but they never think about the business that sold them their set.

Consumer Couch Potatoes laugh at their favorite sitcoms... but they never think about the business that produced or broadcast the show.

As a result, millions of Americans are expert consumers. We know the brand names of dozens of products. We know the slogans and punchlines from hundreds of TV commercials. Why, we're the most consumer-literate country in the world, hands down!

But when it comes to *business knowledge*—well, that's a couch of a different color! Countless hours on the Consumer Couch have conditioned us to spend wealth, not create wealth.

Time to Get off the Consumer Couch

When you joined the Quixtar business, you made the decision to get off the Consumer Couch and become an independent business owner. I applaud your ambition and drive.

But I must warn you that if you're like most people, you've spent tens of thousands of hours on the Consumer

Couch, but relatively few hours as a business owner. Which means because you've had tons of experience as a consumer, you're likely to try to apply your consumer thinking to your business. And that's a disaster waiting to happen!

You see, there's a big difference between sitting on the Consumer Couch watching *The Price Is Right*... and sitting in the business meetings with the owners and producers of the show, making the serious decisions and doing the hard work that has brought the show into your living room five days a week for 30-plus years.

Likewise, there's a big difference between *thinking like a consumer* and buying stuff on sale or at deep discount stores... and *thinking like an independent business owner* and offering quality products for a fair and reasonable price.

In other words, there's a big difference between *consumer-think* and *business owner-think*.

Consumer-think is about spending wealth. Cheap prices. Deep discounts. Getting more stuff for less money. Buying liabilities. And shopping at someone else's store.

Business Owner-think is about creating wealth. Fair prices. Adding value. Building a bigger business and a better person. Investing in assets. And shopping at "Your Store," instead of "Their Store."

In other words, more often than not, consumer-think and business owner-think are opposite sides of the free enterprise coin! Now, that's not necessarily a bad thing.

Using consumer-think to buy more stuff for less money can be a good thing—UNLESS you try to apply consumer-think to the business-think side of the free enterprise coin! That's when the wheels start to fall off your vehicle to time and money freedom.

So, do yourself a BIG favor. Get off the Consumer Couch... walk into your business office... change your thinking from consumer-think to owner-think... and start getting the most out of the Quixtar opportunity!

Understand and Honor Your Business Model

Great minds discuss ideas. Average minds discuss events. Small minds discuss people.

—Admiral Rickover
U.S. Navy

Ever wonder how legendary companies get started? Do they begin with elaborate business plans? Expensive market surveys? Billion-dollar loans?

None of the above.

More often than not, great businesses begin with a great idea and a basic business model that people can easily understand and execute. The founding of Southwest Airlines is a perfect example.

In 1971, a businessman named Rollin King invited his friend and attorney, Herb Kelleher, for dinner at a local restaurant. As they sat talking, King drew a triangle on a cocktail napkin and scribbled down the names of the three biggest cities in Texas at each corner of the triangle.

15

Great businesses begin with a great idea and a basic business model that people can easily understand and execute.

Then he explained to Kelleher how he planned to connect the three cities by a low-fare, no-frills airline that would make flying affordable for everyone. He asked Kelleher to be the company president.

"Rollin, you're crazy!" Kelleher shouted. *"Let's do it!"*

That was the beginning of Southwest Airlines, the nation's most profitable airline over the last 20 years and the business model that changed an entire industry.

Every Business Has a Model

Every business is based on some kind of business model. In the case of Southwest Airlines, the business model is low fares and high volume. In the case of the Concorde, it's just the opposite—high fares and low volume. Same industry, but very different business models. *And they both work!*

When it comes to business models, there's no right model or wrong model, *per se.* There are only models that work. And models that don't work. The key to running a successful business is to find a model that works, and then work that model over and over and over again.

My background is in the hospitality industry (that's the fancy term for hotels and restaurants). There are scores of different business models in the hospitality industry, and each of the models has its success stories. Just look at some of the hotel business models available to travelers in and around Orlando, Florida, where I used to live and teach before we moved to the Miami Beach area:

For starters, there are hundreds of "mom-and-pop" business models, such as independently owned hotels, motels and bed-and-breakfasts. Then there are dozens of business models owned by chains or franchises, beginning with the bare-bones, low-cost motels—such as Motel Six and the like; and ending with the high-cost luxury hotels—such as the exclusive Breakers Hotel in Palm Beach, Florida. Off the top of my head, here's a sampling of some of the more common business models operating in the hospitality industry:

There are *suites-hotel* business models, such as Homestead Suites.

Extended-stay business models, such as The Suburban Lodge.

Theme-park business models, such as The Animal Kingdom Lodge inside Disney World.

Convention hotel business models, such as The Peabody.

Business hotel business models, such as The Hilton.

Mid-priced, family-stay business models, such as Holiday Inn.

Historic hotel business models, such as the century-old Park Avenue Hotel in Winter Park.

Golf and tennis resort business models, such as The Mission Inn in central Florida.

And, last but not least, *luxury hotel* business models, such as the Ritz Carlton and Four Seasons.

I just named nine tried-and-true business models—and *that's in just one industry!* Although the business models above are very different, one model isn't necessarily better than another. Last time I checked, both the Motel Six and Ritz Carlton business models were performing well—yet you'd be hard pressed to find two business models in the hospitality industry with more fundamental differences.

Don't Mix and Match Your Models

As consumers, we don't sit around and analyze different business models. Yet, depending on our wants and needs, we visit dozens of different business models during the course of the week. In fact, there are so many different business models available to consumers today that we take them for granted. Drive down any busy street in any city in North America, and you're likely to see a hundred different business models in a five-mile stretch. Here are just a few common business models you're likely to drive by on your way home from work:

- One-hour dry cleaners
- Discount warehouse
- Doctor's office
- Self-service car wash
- Convenience store
- Consignment clothing shop
- Family restaurant
- Used car lot
- Drive-through fast food
- Pharmacy
- Plumbing service
- Factory-direct furniture store
- Hardware store
- Quick lube and oil change

Now, as consumers, we enter each of these businesses with a certain set of expectations. For example, we expect to sit in the waiting room of the doctor's office for half an hour before we're ushered into a room where we'll wait another 15 minutes before the doctor comes in. But when we steer our car into a McDonald's drive-through, we don't expect to wait half an hour in line, do we? At McDonald's, we expect immediate service or we leave!

> **As consumers, we know better than to mix our business models. I mean, nobody in their right mind would go into a Ritz Carlton and demand a room for the same price as Motel Six**

In other words, as consumers, we know better than to mix our business models. I mean, nobody in their right mind would go into a Ritz Carlton and demand a room for the same price as Motel Six. I doubt if you'll ever have the following conversation at the Ritz:

"Did you just say $279 a night for a room? Excuse me. **Excu-s-s-s-e me!** *Who are you trying to kid? I can get a room down the street at Motel Six for $39.95. I demand the same price!"*

You won't have this conversation because, as a consumer, you intuitively understand that it doesn't make sense to mix business models. In fact, mixing business models can get downright comical. Would you frequent any establishment with these names?

- "Discount Sushi and Bait Shack"
- "Dental Drive-Through"
- "Rent-a-Meal"
- "Self-Help Prescriptions"
- "Facelifts While U Wait"

Let's have a little fun mixing business models. On the left is a list of common business models. On the right is a list of popular products and services. See what kind of zany combinations you can come up with:

New and used...	Water
Discount...	Produce
One-hour...	Funerals
Do-it-yourself...	Church service
Rent to own...	Plumbing
Custom...	Pets
Homemade...	Accounting
Consignment...	Haircuts
24-hour...	Prescriptions
Mobile....	Surgery

I must admit, a couple of the mixed models jumped off the page at me—"custom accounting" and "discount surgery," for example. (Even though "custom accounting" isn't really so far-fetched, considering that's exactly the service that Arthur Andersen accountants performed for Enron and World Com. But that's another story....) But discount surgery?—well, let's not even go there.

Why the Deep-Discount Business Model Doesn't Mix with the Quixtar Business Model

I hope my little exercise brings home the point that it's silly for consumers to mix business models. I mean, if I need surgery, the last thing I'm looking for is discounts! It's more than silly to try to mix surgery and discounts. It's ridiculous! The same can be said for trying to mix the discount-store model with the Quixtar business model—it's ridiculous!

When prospects or new IBOs say things like, *"Why don't you lower the prices in Quixtar and make it a giant discount buying club—then everyone would want to join"*... what they're doing is mixing business models. People mean well when they say things like that. They look at how big Wal-Mart is and how many people shop there, and they jump to an illogical conclusion: "Wal-Mart is the biggest retailer in the world. Wal-Mart has the cheapest prices in the world. Therefore, make Quixtar prices cheaper than Wal-Mart, and everybody will want to buy from you, instead of them."

> **Sam Walton consciously chose the deep-discount model for his chain of retail stores. It was a great choice for Wal-Mart and the Walton family, who are rich beyond belief, thanks to Sam's vision.**

Sounds logical enough, doesn't it?

One problem. People who make statements like this are using consumer-think instead of business-think. As a result, they're trying to mix business models that don't mix! Allow me to elaborate:

Years ago, Wal-Mart's founder, Sam Walton, decided to take a different approach to retailing. Instead of selling *a few products at high prices in one or two local stores,* like most retailers of that era, Walton decided to sell *lots of products at low prices in hundreds of stores in small towns across America.* In order to do that, he had to forsake luxury and service for cheap prices. Sam Walton consciously chose the deep-discount model for his chain of retail stores. It was a great choice for Wal-Mart and the Walton family, who are rich beyond belief, thanks to Sam's vision.

Wal-Mart Is ONE Successful Model, But Not the ONLY Successful Model!

Wal-Mart became so good at working the deep-discount business model that the company became the world's biggest retailer in less than 40 years. No question—today Wal-Mart is the undisputed king of deep-discount!

The key to operating a successful business is to find a business model that works best for your particular business... UNDERSTAND why and how the model works... and then HONOR the model by working it over and over again.

But no one would think of going into a Wal-Mart looking to buy an Armani suit or a Rolex watch, would they? No one would think of going into Wal-Mart for expert advice from their clerks, would they? No one would think of going into Wal-Mart to marvel at their architecture and interior design, would they? Why? Because consumers know that Wal-Mart stands for "everyday low prices." Not luxury. Not great service. Not elegant atmosphere. Just "everyday low prices." Nothing more, nothing less.

The deep-discount business model also works well for Motel Six. But the luxury business model works just great for Ritz Carlton. The key to operating a successful business is to find a business model that works best for your particular

22

business... UNDERSTAND why and how the model works... and then HONOR the model by working it over and over again.

My point is this: The deep-discount business model that Wal-Mart has chosen to follow has proved to be a very successful business model for them. Wal-Mart epitomizes *one* successful business model. But the deep discount model is NOT the *only* successful business model! In fact, it's only *one of hundreds, if not thousands, of business models that work!*

How Prices Are Set

There are two fools in every market: one asks too little, one asks too much.

—Russian proverb

I have a friend who owns a printing company. Over the years he's learned that his customers demand three things: the cheapest price; the best quality; and the quickest turnaround. But it was impossible to give his customers all three benefits and still run a profitable business.

So he posted this sign in the lobby:

Our Company Guarantees...

1) Low cost

2) Quick turnaround

3) Quality

Pick any two!

As a business owner, the printer understood that customers can't have it all—*something's got to give!*

If customers want low cost and quality, then they have to *give up* a quick turnaround.

If they want low cost and a quick turnaround, then they have to *give up* quality.

If they want quick turnaround and quality, then they have to *give up* low cost.

The Definition of Price

Obviously, money is one of the things you have to *give up* to buy goods and services. But it's certainly not the only thing! In the case of the printer, customers may have to give up quality. Or time. Or even more money to get what they want. But rest assured, they have to give up something. And so do you, no matter where you shop!

> **Price is what you have to give up to get what you want. Obviously, money is one of the things you have to give up to buy goods and services. But it's certainly not the only thing!**

Most consumers would define "price" as the amount of money they have to pay for a product or service. But this is a very narrow, consumer-think way of defining price. The printer, on the other hand, had a much broader definition of price. He defined price the way I define it:

Price is what you have to give up to get what you want.

When you shop at Wal-Mart, for example, you may give up less money than when you shop at a Circle K convenience store, a growing franchise with hundreds of stores across the country. But you also have to *give up time* (you have to drive there, park, and walk around their stadium-sized store). You *give up convenience* (wouldn't it be a lot more convenient to order by phone or via the Internet?). And most importantly, you *give up opportunity* (the time you spend shopping at Wal-Mart and traveling to and from the store could be time spent making money, instead of spending money).

When you dash into a Circle K convenience store, on the other hand, you give up more money, but you get some valuable intangibles, which is why the cost of products at convenience stores is higher than discount stores.

The Problem with Price Comparisons

Here's a scene you're not likely to see any time soon:

A person carrying a Wal-Mart flyer walks into a Circle K convenience store and begins making a list comparing the prices of seven products carried at both stores. The completed list looks like this:

Product	Circle K Price	Wal-Mart Price
1. WD 40 (8 oz.)	$3.29	$1.77
2. STP gas treatment (8 oz.)	$1.69	$ .94
3. Purina Dog Chow (4.4 lbs.)	$4.39	$3.38
4. Zephyrhills bottled water (1 gal.)	$1.49	$ .79
5. Maxwell House coffee (4 oz.)	$3.89	$2.19
6. Pepsi 12-pack of cans	$3.29 (on sale)	$2.50
7. Excedrin Extra (24 tablets)	$5.49	$2.96

Then the person asks to see the owner and says:

"You know, I was thinking about buying a Circle K franchise. I was really excited about the opportunity. So I decided to compare your prices to Wal-Mart. Look at this list comparing the two stores. Just look at how much cheaper Wal-Mart prices are than yours. Why would anyone want to shop at your store when they could shop at Wal-Mart? If Circle K would make their prices cheaper than Wal-Mart's, then I would buy a franchise because everyone would want to shop at my store."

Now, the first question most Circle K franchisees would ask is, *"What planet are you from?"* But assuming this owner is a nice guy, he would likely say something like this:

"First of all, people who shop at Circle K aren't shopping for the lowest price. They're shopping for convenience. They're shopping to save time. The nearest Wal-Mart is at least 20 minutes from here when the traffic is light. During rush hour, it's more than an hour away. Our customers don't mind paying 50% more, even 100% more, than Wal-Mart because they understand that their time is priced into our products.

"In fact, I tell my customers that they actually save money shopping at convenience stores rather than Wal-Mart. Why? Because convenience store customers are

> **Prices and business models go hand in hand, which is why the price is right when Wal-Mart charges $1.77 for an 8-ounce can of WD-40. And the price is right when Circle K charges $3.29 for the same product.**

in a hurry. They grab one or two items and they're out the door. The typical retail sale in my store is less than $10. When is the last time you spent less than $10 in a Wal-Mart? When people shop at Wal-Mart, they see thousands of products displayed. They may go into the store with the purpose of buying a pillow, but they leave the store with a pillow, PLUS a comforter, two sets of sheets, a claw hammer, and two videos they'll never get around to watching.

"So, you see, I'm not interested in lowering my prices because I don't have to. In fact, I wish corporate headquarters would raise some prices so that I could have bigger profit margins."

Why the Price Is Right in Both Stores

The lesson to be learned is this: Prices and business models go hand in hand, which is why *the price is right when Wal-Mart charges $1.77* for an 8-ounce can of WD-40. And *the price is right when Circle K charges $3.29* for the same product. Yes, both prices are different, but both prices are exactly right! Asking a higher price for the same product doesn't mean the lower price is right and the higher price is wrong. It just means the business models distributing the product are different.

> **If you can buy a product at a lower price from Store A than Store B, it doesn't mean the lower price is right and the higher price is wrong. Both prices can be right, depending on the business model.**

Now, this is a crucial principle for understanding and honoring the Quixtar business model, so let me repeat this irrefutable business axiom. *If you can buy a product at a lower price from Store A than Store B, it doesn't mean the lower price is right and the higher price is wrong. Both prices can be right, depending on the business model.*

Need another example? Let's compare prices at two major discount stores, Wal-Mart and Target. If you compare identical products at these two stores, Target's prices will be higher 90% of the time. That's a fact.

But guess what—I'd much rather shop at Target than Wal-Mart. Why? Because Target has cleaner stores. Wider aisles. A better product mix. Prettier product displays. More sales clerks. And quicker checkouts. I'm delighted to pay an extra 10% to 20% at Target because, in my opinion, the shopping experience is 100% better!

> **Even deep discounters like Wal-Mart want to sell their products at the highest possible price and still undersell the competition.**

Two Sides of the Pricing Coin

Depending on which side of the business counter you're standing, the word "price" has two different meanings. If you're a consumer, price means the *out-go you have to spend* for products and services. If you're a business owner, price means the *income you receive* for your products and services.

Here's the challenging part of the consumer/business owner transaction. Consumers want to buy products for the least money. Business owners want just the opposite—they want to sell products for the most money they can get. Even deep discounters like Wal-Mart want to sell their products at the highest possible price and still undersell the competition. If every discount store except Wal-Mart suddenly went out of business, what do you think would happen to Wal-Mart's prices? They'd go up across the board, wouldn't they? That's not wrong. That's just business.

When I owned a hotel and a restaurant, for example, I always tried to get the most for my products. I'd price my rooms and my food as high as I could and then try to add as much value as possible to justify my prices.

The Money Pit

People who think they're "shopping smart" by buying at deep discount stores fail to see the big picture. Conditioned to become consumer-thinkers, most people assume that cheaper is better, which is why Wal-Mart is the world's largest retailer, with more than 3,000 stores in 10 countries and $200 billion in annual sales—and growing!

Wal-Mart works the deep-discount model better than anyone. In fact, Wal-Mart's stated goal is to become a one-stop discount shopping mall. That's why Wal-Mart began diversifying into groceries—they knew from research that customers shopping for meat and vegetables are likely to look around and buy higher-profit, non-grocery items, such as electronics. In some parts of the country, Wal-Mart is even experimenting with selling used cars!

Did you ever see a movie called *The Money Pit?* A young couple buys a charming old home with the idea of fixing it up with a few hundred bucks' worth of paint. But once they move in, they encounter one major expense after another. By the end of the movie, the couple has spent 100 times more than they originally intended.

Same goes for shopping at discount stores. Wal-Mart entices people into their stores with loss leaders and low prices with the intention of selling shoppers additional products with higher profit margins. Unsuspecting consumers go in the door intending to "save" money on, say, a gallon of milk and a dozen eggs. But two hours later, they leave wearing a new pair of prescription eyeglasses and driving a "Wal-Mart pre-owned" car. And when they get home, they unload the new DVD player they bought, along with an ironing board and a fishing rod, when they suddenly realize they forgot to buy the milk and eggs! Even non-discount retailers use the "get-'em-in-with-low-prices-and-then-sell-'em-more-stuff" concept to separate unwary consumers from their hard-earned money. That's their business model.

The Garage Sale Inventory Test

Let's face it—shoppers always buy more stuff at the store than they intended to. Considering that the average grocery store stocks 40,000 products, temptations lurk in every aisle. Be honest—have you ever shopped at a Wal-Mart supercenter or Home Depot and NOT come home with something that wasn't on your shopping list?

Hey, high-volume dealers know that consumers are impulsive. That's how they stay in business—by selling shoppers gewgaws and thingamajigs that they can't resist but will seldom use or, more likely, simply don't need.

Now, before you congratulate yourself for being a disciplined shopper who is immune to impulse buying, I want you to take a few minutes and take The Garage Sale Inventory Test.

Take a piece of paper and a pen and open each of the closets in the house. Now, write down the name of the products stored in your closets that you haven't worn or

> **Be honest—have you ever shopped at a Wal-Mart supercenter or Home Depot and NOT come home with something that wasn't on your shopping list?**

used in the last 12 months. Do the same in your kids' rooms... in the hall closet... in the pantry... under the bathroom sinks... under the kitchen counter... and in the garage. Now, once you've jotted down your list, estimate the original price of each item, jot it down, and add up the total. (Bigger number than you thought, isn't it?)

Now ask yourself, "If I had a garage sale tomorrow, which of these items would I put in the sale and what would I charge for each item?" Then circle the garage sale items, write down the price you'd ask, and add up that total. Now compare the two totals. Depressing, isn't it?

I had my wife, Jeanne, take The Garage Sale Inventory Test recently. She came up with a list of 47 items that were garage saleable—and that was just stuff stored in our garage! Sure, we need a bicycle tire pump. But not four of them! We need Christmas decorations. But not a four-foot-tall Santa that swivels his hips while singing *Jingle Bell Rock!* Something tells me "singing santa" was an impulse buy, 'cause it certainly wasn't on any of my shopping lists!

The Quixtar business model, on the other hand, isn't designed to entice people into a store with loss leaders in order to sell people stuff they didn't plan on buying and likely don't need. Unlike discount stores, Quixtar's business model is designed to sell products that really work... to people who really need them... at really fair and reasonable prices. That's a business model worth building.

My point is that our lives are cluttered with stuff that we bought from stores on impulse. Add them up, and these "great deals that we had to have on the spur of the moment" cost us hundreds, if not thousands, of dollars, when we bought them new. What's their total worth at a weekend garage sale (assuming you can find a buyer)? Maybe $29.17, if you're lucky.

It's foolish to try to compete with Wal-Mart by adopting their discount model. The good news is that you don't have to! The key is to do what convenience stores do—adopt a business model that offers intangibles that Wal-Mart can never offer. Such as great service. Convenience. Opportunity. Or, better yet, all three.

When you think about all the money you've thrown away over the years buying stuff on impulse—well, you've gotta laugh. I know one thing for sure... the discount stores that sold you the stuff are laughing too—all the way to the bank!!

The Quixtar business model, on the other hand, isn't designed to entice people into a store with loss leaders in order to sell people stuff they didn't plan on buying and likely don't need. Unlike discount stores, Quixtar's business model is designed to sell products that really work... to people who really need them... at really fair and reasonable prices. That's a business model worth building.

You Can't Be All Things to All People

Now, I don't mean to sound like a Wal-Mart basher. Wal-Mart is the best at what they do. They've perfected the deep-discount business model, and companies that try to compete directly with them on "everyday low prices" are in for trouble. Just ask Kmart, which recently filed for bankruptcy.

It's foolish to try to compete with Wal-Mart by adopting their discount model. *The good news is that you don't have to!* The key is to do what convenience stores do—adopt a business model that offers intangibles that Wal-Mart can never offer. Such as great service. Convenience. Opportunity. Or, better yet, all three.

You've heard the expression, "You can't be all things to all people," haven't you? This axiom especially applies to business models. Wal-Mart understands that they can't be all things to all people. Do you think Wal-Mart cares if patrons of Saks Fifth Avenue wouldn't be caught dead in Wal-Mart? Not on your life.

Just as Wal-Mart executives don't sit around the conference table talking about how to compete with upscale business models like Lord & Taylor and Tiffany's, Wal-Mart's head honchos don't spend their time thinking up ways to turn their customers into independent business owners, either. Why? Because the leadership at Wal-Mart is too busy worrying about their own business

Comparing Quixtar's prices to Wal-Mart's is like comparing Wal-Mart's prices to Circle K's— you're comparing apples to oranges. If you're going to compare, throw in the intangibles of your business model, and you'll see that people get a LOT more intangibles with the Quixtar model than they do with the deep-discount model.

model to worry about Quixtar and Saks and Circle K and the hundreds of other business models operating in the free enterprise system. Instead of worrying about other business models, Wal-Mart sticks to its knitting and continues to work its business model, day in and day out.

Likewise, Quixtar IBOs shouldn't worry themselves about Wal-Mart's prices. Comparing Quixtar's prices to Wal-Mart's is like comparing Wal-Mart's prices to Circle K's—you're comparing apples to oranges. If you're going to compare, throw in the intangibles of your business model, and you'll see that people get a LOT more intangibles with the Quixtar model than they do with the deep-discount model.

Are you beginning to see why price is much more than just dollars and cents... and why prices go hand in hand with business models?

How Businesses Set Prices

Ever notice how prices for goods and services are all over the board? Why does a new Camry cost $20,000 and a new Lexus cost $60,000? Why does Attorney Smith charge $150 an hour, while Attorney Jones charges $500 an hour? Why does a haircut at a barbershop cost $5, while a haircut at a beauty salon costs $25?

At first glance, it would appear that some businesses pull prices right out of the air. True, there's no tried-and-true formula for setting prices. But there are a lot of pricing paradigms that businesses can model their prices after. Here is a list of 10 of the most common pricing models:

1) *Supply and demand* (low supply plus high demand equals high prices)

2) *Competition* (the reason the government accepts the lowest bid)

3) *What the market will bear* (Mr. Market is moody, but he'll always let you know if your prices are way out of line)

4) *Loss leader* (increase traffic by offering a high-demand product below cost, and then sell LOTS of other stuff)

5) *Cost plus* (calculate what it costs to produce a product, then add your profit)

6) *Value-added pricing* (add intangibles to justify the higher price)

7) *Packaging* (dress up a 4" CD-ROM in a 1-foot-square, hyper-decorated box)

8) *Bundling* (give them the razor free, charge a premium for the blades)

9) *Discount pricing* (make up for low prices by selling high volume)

10) *Threshold pricing* (determine the top price in a given category, and then price your product near the very top)

Are you beginning to see why price is much more than just dollars and cents... and why prices go hand in hand with business models? As you go to the next chapter, keep in mind the definition of price: *Price is what you have to give up to get what you want.* (Which means the *less* you give up in money, the *more* you must give up in intangibles.)

In the next chapter we're going to go one step further and see how Quixtar prices are set, and, more importantly, how those prices include intangibles that make Quixtar products the best value in the world!

How Quixtar Prices Are Set

In the market economy, the price that is offered is counted upon to produce the wealth that is sought.

—John Kenneth Galbraith
economist

H ere's an old joke that illustrates how arbitrary prices can be.

A gorilla walks into an ice cream parlor, sits down at the counter, and orders a banana split. The owner is shocked to see a gorilla in his shop, but he quickly realizes that this is a rare opportunity to make some quick money.

As the owner slices up the bananas, he's thinking about what he can charge for the banana split.

"Gorillas aren't too smart," the owner says to himself. *"He's probably on leave from the zoo and doesn't get around very much. I bet I can charge him 10 times the normal price and he won't know the difference."*

The owner sets the banana split on the counter and steps back to watch as the gorilla begins to eat with gusto. The owner smiles as he writes up the bill.

"Like taking candy from a baby," he thinks to himself as he slides the bill toward the gorilla. The gorilla frowns as he looks at the bill, then pulls out two $20-dollar bills and hands them to the owner.

Plucking the bills from the gorilla's huge hand, the owner attempts to engage the gorilla in some light conversation.

"I must say I was a bit startled to see you. We don't get many gorillas in here."

"Can't say I'm surprised," the gorilla replies. *"Forty dollars is a lot of money for a banana split."*

Silly story—but what does it have to do with Quixtar prices? Well, first of all, the story points out that prices are relative, because businesses price their goods and services according to what the market will bear. Now don't get me wrong—I'm not advocating that you act like the owner of the ice cream parlor and gouge innocent people (or innocent gorillas, for that matter). Price gouging is not only unethical, it's also illegal, so obviously, that's not the best way to set prices.

But as a business professor, I do say that prices are relative, not absolute. The prices of a product, including banana splits, can vary tremendously from one business to another. And that's perfectly legal and legitimate. Not only are different prices for the same product okay, relative pricing is the rule in the marketplace, rather than the exception. We talked about this phenomenon earlier in the book when we compared the prices of products at a supermarket and a convenience store.

Crash Course in Economics 101

Now it's time to examine in more depth the economic realities that determine prices. Let's start our discussion by analyzing the pricing of the product in this chapter's opening story—a banana split.

Last time I checked, a banana split at the local Dairy Queen cost about $4, tax included. The same banana split at an ice cream parlor in Disney World would cost you at least twice as much—$8, or more. And a banana split delivered to your room at the Ritz Carlton in Tokyo would cost about the same as the gorilla's—$40!

To make profits, business owners must first retire variable costs... then use the money left over (the contribution margin) to contribute to paying off the fixed costs. The money that remains is pure profit.

How can a business justify charging customers $40, or even $8, for that matter, for a product that contains maybe 50 cents' worth of ingredients and is priced less than $4 at the local Dairy Queen? Follow along as I deliver a brief lesson in Economics 101.

Let's start by talking about how profits are made. The word *profit* refers to the money left over after all the *costs* of running a business (the outgo) are deducted from the gross revenue (the income). Businesses incur two kinds of costs—**variable** costs and **fixed costs.**

Variable costs are expenses associated with producing and marketing a product. These costs *vary* because the more products a company sells, the more products the company has to manufacture or buy.

Fixed costs are expenses associated with the overhead. Fixed costs (such as monthly rent) stay basically the same, whether the company sells more stuff or not.

The profit equation for the ice cream parlor in the opening story would look something like this:

Profit = Gross Revenue – (Variable Costs + Fixed Costs)

Below is a list of the ice cream parlor's basic variable and fixed costs:

Variable Costs	Fixed Costs
Ice cream	Rent
Cones, bowls, utensils	Electricity, water
Soda	Appliances & furnishings
Toppings	
Advertising	
Labor	

In order to make a profit, the ice cream parlor must first pay off all of the *variable costs* (the costs associated with making and marketing the banana splits). The money left over after paying off the variable costs is called the **contribution margin** because it *contributes* to paying off the *fixed costs*. Once the fixed costs are retired, the money left over is the owner's profit.

The way I explain this concept to my students it to tell them to think of fixed costs as a hole in the ground. Each day the hole must be filled up before a business can start making a profit.

For example, imagine a company that buys widgets for $4 each (variable cost) and resells them for $10 each (selling price). This leaves a $6 contribution margin ($10 - $4 VC = $6 CM).

Let's say the company's fixed costs are $600 a day. Each time a widget is sold, the company deposits $6 into the fixed cost hole. The company must drop $6 into the hole 100 times a day to break even. After 100 widgets are sold, the profit pile will grow in $6 increments until the next work day, when the cycle starts all over again.

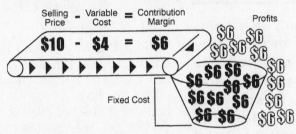

Let's review these key terms again, because understanding the relationship between costs and profits is the key to running every successful business. *To make profits, business owners must first* **retire variable costs**... *then use the money left over (the* **contribution margin***) to contribute to* **paying off the fixed costs**. *The money that remains is pure* **profit**.

In order to understand why "the price is right" for a $4 banana split at Dairy Queen and an $8 banana split at Disney World, you must first understand variable costs, fixed costs, and contribution margin. A glance at the chart below explains why *the $4 price and the $8 price for the same product are BOTH RIGHT.*

Variable Costs Of Banana Split	Fixed Costs @ Local Dairy Queen	Fixed Costs @ Disney World
About the same for both businesses	Several *thousand* per month	*Tens of millions per month!*

Now, remember what has to happen to make a profit? *A business must retire the variable costs and the money left over (the contribution margin) contributes to the fixed costs. What's left is profit, correct?* Well, for both businesses, the variable costs are about the same. *But look at the difference in fixed costs! Disney World's monthly fixed costs are 10,000 times more than the local Dairy Queen!* So, in order to make a profit, Disney has to charge MUCH MORE than Dairy Queen.

For every business, no matter how big or small, the key to profitability is to keep prices at a fair and reasonable level while keeping variable costs down.

So, then, why doesn't Disney charge 10,000 times more than Dairy Queen? Because no one is going to pay $40,000 for a banana split—*not even a dumb gorilla!* So, Disney has to set a fair and reasonable price according to what the market will bear.

Now, if you've ever visited Disney World, it won't take you long to realize that the market at Disney will certainly bear a higher price than the market at the local Dairy Queen. Why? Well, for one, once you're inside Disney World, there's no competition, so Disney is free to set higher prices. Plus, people visiting Disney are not there to save money—they're there to create special memories, and if it costs two or three times more for a banana split to create those memories, so be it!

As for the $40 banana split at the Tokyo Ritz Carlton, because Japan has a closed economy and because it's a relatively small island nation that must import almost all of its natural resources, such as oil, the variable costs and fixed costs are MUCH HIGHER in Tokyo than in the states. As a result, the prices of ALL products and services in Japan are some of the highest in the world.

Now are you beginning to see why I say "the price is right," even if the price of a product is MUCH higher at Business A than Business B?

Quixtar Corporate Costs

Now let's see how variable costs, fixed costs, and contribution margin affect the Quixtar product line, as well as your independent business. Let's begin by listing the variable costs and fixed costs for Quixtar Corporate.

Quixtar Corporate

Variable Costs	*Fixed Costs*
Manufacturing	Buildings
Shipping & distribution	Equipment
Warehousing	Administration offices
Transportation	Computers & office equipment
Raw materials & ingredients	Utilities
Product packaging	Administrative payroll
	Research & development
	Intl. expansion
	Website development & support

Given that Quixtar Corporate is a multi-billion-dollar corporation, it's obvious that the variable and fixed costs are enormous, averaging hundreds of millions of dollars every year. For every business, no matter how big or small, the key to profitability is to keep prices at a fair and reasonable level while keeping variable costs down. But this is

Compared to most businesses, the cost of doing business as a Quixtar IBO is ridiculously small, especially given the upside profit potential.

especially true for a company the size of Quixtar, which aims for *profits that run into the hundreds of millions, if not billions, of dollars each year—and these profits are shared with you!* You can't have profit sharing without profits—so, the more profits Quixtar Corporate makes, the more profits that are available to IBOs. Which means you don't just want Quixtar to have profits every year. You want them to have RECORD profits every year so that you can position yourself to enjoy record profits in your business each and every year!

Compare Your Costs to Convenience Stores

Now, here's the best part of the Quixtar profit picture. Quixtar Corporate assumes the lion's share of the variable and fixed costs associated with the Quixtar opportunity. Compared to most businesses, the cost of doing business as a Quixtar IBO is ridiculously small, especially given the upside profit potential.

Take a moment to compare the two charts below, which show the monthly variable and fixed costs for a typical IBO, as compared to the start-up costs for the owner of a Circle K franchise, a business model that we've talked about previously in this book.

Quixtar IBO

Variable Costs	Fixed Costs
Literature	Computer
Product samples	Home office
Cost of product for retailing	Office phone lines
Gas for car	Monthly books, tapes, tools
	Internet service provider (ISP)

Start-up Costs for Circle K Franchise*

Expenditure	Low-High Range
Franchise fee	$ 15,000
Training expenses	$ 2,000-12,000
Building construction	$175,000-600,000
Equipment & signage	$115,000-195,000
Site development costs	$120,000-150,000
Deposits & licenses	$ 3,500-24,000
Inventory	$ 30,000-70,000
Grand opening costs	$ 5,000-10,000
Insurance	$ 4,500-12,000
Professional fees	$ 1,000-5,000
Additional costs	$ 10,000-20,000
Total	$481,000 - 1,113,000

*from circlek.com website
© 2000-2002 Tosco Corporation

> **The key to success in business isn't the lowest prices; rather, it's finding a business model that works, and then working that model over and over again.**

As I said, the out-of-pocket expenses above are *just the start-up costs* for a Circle K franchise! Investors have to pay off these start-up costs PLUS their monthly variable and fixed costs before they begin making dime one in profit!

Compare that to the Quixtar opportunity. A Quixtar IBO could operate a profitable business for an entire year for what it costs a Circle K franchisee *each day!* Yet, despite the huge start-up costs and massive monthly overhead, convenience store franchises are selling like hotcakes. Why? Because even though their prices are 20% to 200% higher than Wal-Mart's, the owners of well-located convenience stores are making money. Just goes to show you that the key to success in business isn't the lowest prices; rather, it's finding a business model that works, and then working that model over and over again.

Why Lower Prices Lead to Lower Profits

As a consultant to the hospitality industry, I'm constantly reminded of the fact that Americans have been conditioned to think cheaper is better. For example, whenever I'm asked to help a struggling restaurant or hotel, every now and then an inexperienced owner will say, *"I've cut my prices as low as I can, and I still can't make a profit."*

When I hear that, the first thing I do is pull out a pen, grab a cocktail napkin, and give the guy a brief napkin presentation explaining why cutting prices is usually the WORST strategy to increase profits. Here's the napkin presentation I call "the profit box."

The Profit Box

Full price	Lower price 20%
Product price = $10	Product price = $8
$5 contribution margin	$3 contribution margin
$5 costs	$5 costs

Once I draw these boxes, I explain that when prices are lowered, *the costs stay the same* because the owner still has to buy food, pay rent, pay employees, etc. Those costs remain $5. If the costs remain the same, then what goes down when the price is lowered is the contribution margin, correct?

That's bad enough, but what most people overlook is how *severely* the contribution margin is affected by discounts. When the price goes down 20%—from $10 to $8—*the contribution margin goes down 40%—from $5 to $3!* (Do the math: $5 – $3 = $2, which is 40% of the original $5 contribution margin.)

At this point, the owner usually slumps his shoulders and says something like, "Yeah, but I hoped to make up the loss of contribution margin by increasing sales."

Great idea!" I say. "But how many more sales do you think you'd need to make up for the lost revenue?"

"Well, if I lower the price by 20%, then obviously I'll have to sell 20% more meals."

Sounds logical, doesn't it? But this is why it's so important to understand contribution margin. The owner is right in assuming that he'll have to sell more meals. But he's always shocked to learn that it's not 20% more. Or even 40% more. Truth is, *if the prices are discounted 20%, the owner will have to sell 67% more meals to get back to square one!* Follow along as I do the math:

The contribution margin (CM) on a $10 meal = $5
100 meals = $500 CM

The contribution margin (CM) on an $8 meal = $3
100 meals = $300 CM

How many meals yielding a CM of $3 would you have to sell to make up the $200 difference? About 67 additional meals (67 x $3 CM = $201). In short, the owner who discounts a $10 meal 20% would have to sell 67% more meals just to get back to where he was before the discounts!

Now are you beginning to see why I say lower prices usually lead to lower profits?

It's Easier (and Smarter) to Increase Value Than to Lower Prices

Okay, we've established that lowering prices in Quixtar leads to lower profits, a scenario that neither the IBOs nor Quixtar Corporate wants to happen. But, some consumer-think people reading this book might respond with this statement:

> **Truth is, if the prices are discounted 20%, the owner will have to sell 67% more meals to get back to square one!**

"Yes, I agree that lowering prices will lower profits. But if the prices are lower, more people will want to buy Quixtar products, so the profits will either stay the same or increase."

Now, I can see why some people would make a statement like that. At first glance, it seems pretty logical. But as I pointed out in the Profit Box story, you'd have to do 67%

more business volume in order to make up for a 20% reduction in price. Think about what this means for your business—if Quixtar Corporate were to reduce its prices 20% across the board, *you'd have to see 67% more people in order to make the same money! Do you have the time for that? NO WAY!*

Look, I understand that Wal-Mart has become one of the great business success stories in history by selling lots of stuff at low prices. But again I remind you that the deep discount business model is *ONE business model, not the ONLY business model!* It works for Wal-Mart, but it's certainly not a fail-proof business model, as the recent bankruptcy of Kmart proves. Yes, Wal-Mart has been able to increase profits by increasing sales. But that's THEIR business model, and it took them 40 years and 3,000 stores to perfect that model.

But as an independent business owner, you must remind clients and prospects of the definition of price—"price is what you have to give up to get what you want." When people shop at Wal-Mart, they have to give up valuable intangibles, such as convenience, service, information, time, and on and on. On the other hand, when people shop at Quixtar.com, all of these great intangibles are added into the price, PLUS they receive the benefit of an unparalleled low-exposure, potentially high-profit business. Can't say that about Wal-Mart, can you?

> **If Quixtar Corporate were to reduce its prices 20% across the board, you'd have to see 67% more people in order to make the same money! Do you have the time for that?**

Understand and Honor Your Business Model

Have you ever noticed that there's a convenience store on every busy street corner? Ever wonder why most convenience stores sell gas, as well as premium-priced groceries? Here's a brief history lesson on the evolution of the convenience store business model:

Are you old enough to remember when gas stations were called service stations? In the 1950s and '60s, you'd pull into a service station and get gassed up without ever having to leave the car! It was great! An attendant would wash your windows and check the oil as he pumped the gas. But service stations gradually gave way to self-serve gas stations, as people sought to save a buck or two per tank by pumping their own gas. Problem was, gas companies soon realized that the profit margins from selling only gas were pitifully small. So they started stocking their small gas stations with high-priced snacks.

> **Instead of continuing to lower prices, the oil companies began adding value—they began offering groceries as an added value to their time-stressed customers.**

It didn't take long for the oil companies' bean counters to recognize that selling premium-priced groceries was far more profitable than selling low-margin gas. So oil companies did an about face and began concentrating on the convenience store part of their businesses. That's why today you see bigger and bigger convenience stores located on more and more high-traffic corners. Exxon... Conoco Mobil... Amoco... Texaco... British Petroleum—they all own convenience store chains, and they're scrambling to build new stores or they're tearing down small, out-dated stores to build bigger, more profitable mega-convenience stores. Do you think the franchisees of the new mega-convenience stores are lowering their prices to compete with the discount stores? Not on your life! The owners are keeping their prices just as high as ever, PLUS, they're continuing to add other high-margin products and services, such as drive-through car washes.

If oil companies can generate enormous profits by adding just one time-saving value, convenience, then just think what you can do by adding not only convenience, but information... one-of-a-kind products... iron-clad guarantees... 24/7 online ordering... delivery to your door... and, above all, OPPORTUNITY!

Here's my point. Years ago oil companies discovered that their deep discount model wasn't working. They had cut their profit margins so low that their gas stations were barely profitable. *So, instead of continuing to lower prices, the oil companies began adding value*—they began offering groceries as an added value to their time-stressed customers. Once the oil companies abandoned their deep-discount model in favor of the convenience store model, profits started pouring in again.

Quixtar's Added Value Really Adds Up!

What lesson can Quixtar IBOs learn from the oil companies? Ponder this. If oil companies can generate enormous profits by adding just one time-saving value, convenience, then just think what you can do by adding not only convenience, but information... one-of-a-kind products... iron-clad guarantees... 24/7 online ordering... delivery to your door... and, above all, OPPORTUNITY!

Folks, think about what you've got here! Forget about low prices. Forget about deep discounts. Convenience stores forgot about those things long ago and concentrated on adding value instead. And they're going like gangbusters!

You can do the same. Just as convenience stores set their prices to make a profit, Quixtar Corporate sets fair and reasonable prices so that they can make a profit—and then they pass a sizeable portion of that profit along to you to compensate you for your efforts in distributing the products and growing your business. Don't question prices. The prices are fine. Quixtar products are priced to sell and priced for profit.

Let your corporate partners do their job of setting prices and adding products, while you go about doing your job of setting appointments and adding value. So, as a business professor and business owner, my advice to you is simple:

Focus on profits, not prices.

That's what Wal-Mart does.

That's what convenience stores do.

And that's what successful IBOs do.

Market the Monsters!

*The best time, place, and manner to sell a
product is any that sells the product.*

—George F. Will
conservative columnist

Early in 2000, Procter & Gamble, the 165-year-old consumer-products giant, was in trouble. Despite investing hundreds of millions of dollars trying to produce a new blockbuster product, the company's sales were flat and the stock price plunged 50%.

Enter A.G. Lafley, the new CEO. Under Lafley, P&G returned to its roots and began concentrating on marketing and extending its well-known core products for home, health, and beauty, including established brands such as Tide detergent, Charmin tissue, Folgers coffee and Crest toothpaste, to name a few.

The result? P&G is back on track, enjoying record profits and solid growth, despite the fact that P&G is a mature company operating in a weak global economy.

Cut a Bigger Slice of the Profit-Pie

There's a valuable lesson that IBOs can learn from the turnaround at P&G: For maximum profitability, *concentrate on marketing the core products that make you the most money.*

In other words, "market the margin monsters," which is the advice I give my clients in the restaurant business. (When I use the phrase "margin monsters," I'm referring to *contribution margin,* which, as we learned in the last chapter, is the money left over after retiring variable costs.) Marketing the monsters means identifying the products with the biggest contribution margins, and then marketing them like mad by building their value, promoting their uniqueness, and constantly keeping them in front of your clients.

> **For maximum profits, you have to identify the products with the highest contribution margins and then aggressively market them to yourself and others.**

For example, a fellow consultant told me how he helped a restaurant in a legendary Florida hotel increase net profits by *several thousand dollars a month* by implementing two simple suggestions to market their margin monsters. When the restaurant manager told the consultant that only 10% of the guests were ordering desserts (which have enormous contribution margins because the ingredients are so inexpensive), the consultant suggested placing the desserts on a rolling display cart and then moving the cart throughout the restaurant every 15 minutes so that the guests would see the desserts while they dined.

Although sales of desserts immediately doubled to 20%, many diners were still turning down dessert because, in the diners' words, "All the desserts look so good that I can't decide." So the consultant suggested adding a "sampler dessert plate" that featured a small slice of each of the desserts. Amazingly, orders for desserts quickly doubled again to 40% of the dinner guests, and a big slice of those increased high-margin sales went straight to the restaurant's bottom line. Now, that's what I call *marketing the margin monsters!*

Nothing But Pancakes

The same concept applies to your Quixtar business—for maximum profits, you have to identify the products with the highest contribution margins and then aggressively market them to yourself and others. Remember, now that you're in business, you have to trade in your consumer-think for business-owner think. And business owners who want to stay in business make business decisions that promote growth and profitability, and marketing the monsters is the surest way to accomplish both goals.

While I was in college, I worked for a small restaurant in Ocean City, New Jersey. Although the restaurant was open for breakfast, lunch, and dinner, a disproportionate share of the profits came from breakfast meals because the contribution margin on eggs, toast, and pancakes was so much higher than foods served during lunch and dinner.

I remember the owner telling me that if it were up to him, he'd serve nothing but pancakes. Why? Because the contribution margin on a $2 stack of pancakes was about $1.80! In other words, it only cost the owner 20 cents in variable costs (pancake mix and water) to make a $2 order of pancakes, which meant the return was NINE TIMES the variable costs! For the owner, pancakes wasn't just a margin monster—it was Godzilla!

Unfortunately for the owner, he was limited to selling his leading margin monster to a few hours every day.

Fortunately for you, you don't have any limitations on marketing your margin monsters. You and your organization can market your monsters every hour of every day!

Managing Your Merchandise Mix

Every successful business has an effective merchandise mix, which is nothing more than the full array of products and services that a business offers. Smart business owners know which products have the highest contribution margins; consequently, they market those products most aggressively. For example, restaurant research reveals that when Americans open their menus, the first place they look is the upper right-hand corner of the right-hand page. So, what do smart restaurant owners do? They advertise their margin monsters in the upper right-hand corner, of course. It only makes good business sense, doesn't it?

So, have you identified the margin monsters in your merchandise mix? In case you didn't know, the margin monsters in your business are the products manufactured by your corporate partner, Quixtar. Just as Tide and the other brand name items represent the core products of P&G, Quixtar-manufactured products make up the core products of your business.

> **By labeling each product with a PV/BV number, corporate gives IBOs a paint-by-numbers system for managing their merchandise mix.**

The products from your partner stores are part of your product mix, and they help your business by expanding your product line. But products from partner stores have a lot less contribution margin than Quixtar's core product line. In fact, on average, *Quixtar products have two-and-a-half times more contribution margin than partner-store products.* The reason is simple. The contribution margin of Quixtar products is high because the company only has to cover its variable costs. But when Quixtar buys products from other companies, it not only has to charge a price that covers their variable costs, *but the price must also cover their fixed costs and their profits,* which means there is a lot less money left to pass along to IBOs.

The Quixtar Paint-by-Numbers Merchandise Mix

Now, I'd like to remind you again that as a business consultant, I've looked at hundreds of businesses over the last 20 years, and I'd say that fewer than 10% can identify their margin monsters. Most business owners assume that the highest-priced products are the most profitable. But that's just not the case! As you now know, the products with the highest contribution margin are the most profitable, which is the reason so many restaurants that do lots of business still manage to lose money. In effect, these restaurants *sell themselves into failure because they don't understand contribution margin.* What a pity!

But now that you understand the importance of contribution margin, you're in a better position to appreciate how Quixtar has designed your business model so that you can easily identify your margin monsters, and, therefore, adjust your merchandise mix to ensure maximum profits. You see, Quixtar Corporate not only understands contribution margin, it also understands how to incentify IBOs to market the margin monsters. How? *By assigning PV/BV numbers to each product!*

PV/BV numbers enable IBOs to instantly identify each product's contribution margin. The higher the PV/BV, the higher the contribution margin. And the higher the contribution margin, the more profitable the product is for both IBOs and Quixtar Corporate. By labeling each product with a PV/BV number, corporate gives IBOs a paint-by-numbers system for managing their merchandise mix. PV/BV numbers take the guesswork out of your marketing strategies. Unlike my restaurant clients, you have no need to pay high-priced consultants to redesign your merchandise mix because the PV/BV numbers are staring you right in the face!

From Good to Great

Now, here's the best part of your paint-by-numbers merchandise mix. As of 2002, Quixtar manufactures more than 450 different top-quality, high-demand, environmentally friendly, health-enhancing products, most of which are consumables. Which means that not only are the core products margin monsters, but they also improve people's lives. And let's face it, very few companies can make that claim!

> **Marketing the monsters is NOT about forsaking the partner stores. It's about focusing on the core products.**

For example, insurance companies have a long history of padding their profits by paying their salespeople bigger commissions to sell the highest-margin products. Nothing wrong with that. Incentifying a sales force with high commissions is good. Unfortunately, all too many of the high-margin insurance products—such as whole life insurance policies with sky-high premiums and sea-level low returns—are as bad for people's fiscal health as desserts and pancakes are bad for their *physical health*. And that's bad!

But Quixtar's margin monsters are not only good for Quixtar Corporate and for IBOs, *they're also good for everyone who uses them!* That's not just good—"THAT'S

GR-R-R-EAT!," as the marketing icon Tony the Tiger would say.

Don't Ignore the Partner Stores

Now, some readers may mistake my suggestion to market the monsters as a plea to ignore the products from the partner stores. That's not where I'm coming from. Marketing the monsters is *NOT about forsaking* the partner stores. It's *about focusing* on the core products.

For example, when I advise my restaurant clients to advertise their margin monsters in the upper right-hand corner of their menus, I'm not suggesting they sell *only* those products. That would be insane! If a restaurant's margin monsters are pasta dishes and some customers don't want pasta for dinner because they had it for lunch, then for heaven's sake, take their order for a different menu item—and serve it with a smile!

Likewise, marketing the monsters in Quixtar means promoting the core products FIRST—and then following up by marketing the partner store products and building the value of the Quixtar shopping experience by emphasizing at-your-door delivery... the option of point-and-click or phone ordering... and no-questions-asked money-back

> **Now that you're a business owner, you have to constantly remind yourself to think like a business owner, not a consumer. And business owner-think tells you that when you market the margin monsters, you and your organization can earn two-and-one-half times more money for the same amount of work.**

guarantees. (No receipt? No problem, unlike most discount and department stores that are refusing cash-back returns without a receipt.)

Make no mistake about it—partner stores are an important part of your product mix. Access to thousands of name-brand products from hundreds of blue chip partner stores is a big feather in your merchandising cap.

But now that you're a business owner, you have to constantly remind yourself to think like a business owner, not a consumer. And business owner-think tells you that when you market the margin monsters, you and your organization can earn two-and-one-half times more money for the same amount of work.

Earning more than twice as much money for the same amount of time and effort—that's what I call working smarter, not harder. And that's what pro-suming in Quixtar is all about!

Home Ownership: Business-Think in Action

In love of home, the love of country has its rise.

—Charles Dickens
from "The Old Curiosity Shop" (1840)

H ere are some lifestyle facts from around the world that remind us how easy it is to draw irrational conclusions.

- The Japanese eat *very little fat* and suffer fewer heart attacks than the British or Americans.

- The French eat *lots of fat,* yet they also suffer fewer heart attacks than the British or Americans.

- The Chinese drink *very little red wine* and suffer fewer heart attacks than the British or Americans.

- While the Italians *drink lots of red wine,* yet they also suffer fewer heart attacks than the British or Americans.

Conclusion: *Eat and drink what you like. It's speaking English that will kill you!*

Enduring Myth about Shopping for Discounts

We laugh at the conclusion that speaking English will kill you because it's such a ridiculous *non sequitur,* a Latin phrase meaning "it does not follow." (The lousy logic makes for a good joke, though.)

While no rational person would arrive at the conclusion that speaking English is bad for your heart, all of us draw irrational conclusions from time to time. For example, according to Dr. Dan Ariely, a consumer research expert at the University of California at Berkeley, most people don't consider themselves irrational. Yet his tests indicate that virtually everyone is irrational when it comes to making money decisions.

Take Dr. Ariely's quiz below to see if you are a rational thinker when it comes to your buying decisions:

Quiz 1: To Save or Not to Save

Circle your answer to each of the following questions:

A) You enter a Body Shop store to buy soap for $7. The salesperson tells you the same soap is on sale for $3 at another Body Shop store, a 10-minute walk away. Would you walk to the other store?

YES   NO

B) You enter a Saks Fifth Avenue store to buy a suit for $677. The salesperson tells you the same suit is on sale for $673 at another Saks store, a 10-minute walk away. Would you walk to the other store?

YES   NO

According to Dr. Ariely, most respondents answer YES to question A and NO to question B. Why? Because they reason that buying $7 soap for $3 represents more than a 50% discount, whereas "saving" $4 on a $677 item represents less than a 1% discount; therefore, they reason, a 50% discount is worth a 10-minute walk, whereas a 1% discount isn't. But as Dr. Ariely points out, $4 is $4, regardless of how expensive the item is. So a rational person would answer either YES to both questions or NO to both questions.

The Only Way to "Save" on Spending Is to Save the Difference

What about you—what was your answer? I answered NO to both questions because I understand that price is what you have to give up to get what you want, and in both cases, it's just not worth my giving up 20 minutes of my life (I'd have to walk to the other store and back) to "save" $4.

In fact, I'll go one step further than Dr. Ariely and say that most people don't "save" when they shop for discounts because their spending creates out-go, not income. When people buy a $10 item on sale for $6, they rationalize that the purchase "saved" them $4. But that's irrational thinking, because when they spend $6, they spend $6. End of discussion! The only way people can literally save by buying at discount is to purchase only the things they really need... and then depositing the difference

> **When people buy a $10 item on sale for $6, they rationalize that the purchase "saved" them $4. But that's irrational thinking, because when they spend $6, they spend $6. End of discussion!**

65

between the retail price and the discount price in a separate bank account and letting it accumulate—*now, that's saving!*

A classic example of pro-suming is buying your own home. You're better off buying a home with a monthly mortgage payment of $1,000 than renting an apartment for $500, a 50% discount that "saves" you $500 a month.

But let's face it, very few people have the discipline to set aside the money they "save" shopping at discount. When people boast to me about how much money they "save" by shopping smart, I say, "Great! But let me ask you a question. If you're such a smart shopper, where is the money you 'saved' at the end of the year?" They usually mumble something like, "I don't really have the money I saved shopping at discount. I spent it buying other stuff on sale." Which means they didn't really "save" money, they just spread around their spending by purchasing even more stuff at discount. Doesn't take a genius to understand why Americans are carrying record amounts of credit card debt, does it?

Pro-suming: Trapping Money in Your Bank Account

In my book *Pro-sumer Power!,* I made the statement that producers make money, consumers spend money, and *pro-sumers make money while they spend.* How do they do that? By buying smarter, instead of cheaper.

A classic example of pro-suming is buying your own home. You're better off buying a home with a monthly mortgage payment of $1,000 than renting an apartment for $500, a 50% discount that "saves" you $500 a month.

Why? Because when you rent, the money you spend *decreases your net worth,* whereas when you own a home in a good neighborhood, the money you spend *increases your net worth.* This is the essence of pro-suming—finding vehicles that empower you to make money while you spend money.

Before we talk about how the Quixtar business model expands the concept of pro-suming to include not just your house, but virtually EVERYTHING in your household, let's take a few minutes to explore the enormous advantages of pro-suming by way of home ownership.

Home Ownership: Business-Owner Think in Action

Why is home ownership such a great deal? For three reasons. One, mortgage payments are like forced savings. Because a portion of your monthly mortgage payment goes toward your principle, *money is automatically trapped* in your home's market value, steadily adding to your personal net worth. Two, any *investments you make in your home can pay huge dividends.* Investing, say, $20,000 in renovations and room additions, can result in a return of two, three, even ten times the original costs. And three, *you can deduct the mortgage interest* from your annual income tax, saving you thousands of dollars a year, year in and year out.

> **When all is said and done, it just makes good business sense to own a home because the financial incentives are so huge.**

When all is said and done, it just makes good business sense to own a home because the financial incentives are so huge. For example, if you rent for 10 years and decide to move, how much money could you put in your pocket for the 120 months of rent? Zero. But if you own a home in a good neighborhood and sell it after 10 years, how much money could you put in your pocket from the sale? Thousands of dollars, or more likely, tens of thousands... and if you were lucky enough (or smart enough) to buy the right home in the right location in a booming market, *you could profit hundreds of thousands—even millions—on the sale of your home!*

When it comes to home ownership, Americans have learned to trade their consumer-think for business-owner think.

Every day millions of people profit from the money trapped in their homes by selling or refinancing, which is why home ownership is one of the cornerstones of the free enterprise system. And it's also why 68% of Americans own their own homes. Even though fewer than 10% of Americans own their own businesses, when it comes to home ownership, Americans have learned to trade their consumer-think for business-owner think. In other words, most American homeowners think like business owners when it comes to making decisions regarding their homes, which is why I say home ownership is business-owner think in action.

Smart Homeowners Think Like Business Owners

What do I mean when I say that "homeowners trade their consumer-think for business-owner think" when it comes to making decisions about their homes, which, for most Americans, is BY FAR their single biggest asset?

It's my observation that most people make good, sound business decisions when it comes to homeownership, including the major decision to own rather than rent (even though owning can cost hundreds, or even thousands, more dollars a month than renting). Although only two out of every three people own a home, I've got to believe the other one-third would own if they could. People rent NOT because they want to—but because they HAVE TO. Either they don't have enough money for a down payment, or they have bad credit or a low-paying job. Let's face it, if conditions were right, I bet 99% of the population would own their own home because the rational, business-think reasons for owning are just too overwhelming to ignore. Homeownership is a no-brainer if there ever was one.

Now, let's take a closer look at the reasons behind homeownership, for those reasons reveal that *virtually everyone has a capacity for making rational, business-think decisions, because they make those decisions day in and day out as homeowners!* For example, let's say a young husband and wife with a family on the way are looking to buy their first home. They have enough income to qualify for a $100,000 loan. They find a well-maintained, three-bedroom, two-bath home built by a reputable builder in a quiet neighborhood with good schools. They discover the exact, same well-maintained model built by the same builder in a different part of town for only $60,000. That's a 40% savings. But remember, price is what you have to give up to get what you want. And buying the $60,000 house means giving up good schools, rapid appreciation, and a crime-free neighborhood.

Most Homeowners Buy Smarter, Not Cheaper

Now, here's where business-think comes into play for homeowners. Research shows that most people buy the most expensive house they can afford! Which means in the above scenario, 90% of buyers would opt for the $100,000 home, as opposed to the $60,000 home! This proves that when it comes to homeownership, people put on their business-think hats and make rational decisions to create wealth by buying smarter, not cheaper. In other words, virtually every homeowner acts like a business owner when it comes to making decisions about their homes.

> **When it comes time to buy a home, the innate, business-think part of people's brains are unconsciously switched on. It's as if the rational, business-think gene lies dormant until it's time to make a homeowner buying decision.**

What this tells me is that people have more business ability than they give themselves credit for! When it comes time to buy a home, the innate, business-think part of people's brains are unconsciously switched on. It's as if the rational, business-think gene lies dormant until it's time to make a homeowner buying decision. When that time comes, the business-think gene is unconsciously switched on until it's time to buy stuff that goes in the home, at which time the business-think gene is unconsciously switched off and the consumer-think gene takes over.

Yo, people! It's time to take conscious control of your business-think switch and turn it on FULL TIME when you're making decisions regarding your Quixtar business. You see, the principles that make home ownership a no-brainer also apply to the Quixtar business. In fact, there's a perfect parallel between the principles that drive the desire for homeownership and the principles that drive the

Quixtar business opportunity. Take a look at how the advantages of the homeowner business model match up with the Quixtar business model:

Home Ownership Principle #1: *A percentage of your monthly mortgage payment is automatically trapped in your home.* You can apply this same principle to your Quixtar business. When you buy Quixtar products for your personal use, buy them through a separate business account. When you keep the difference between the retail price and the wholesale price in your account, you're trapping money in your business, just as you do when you pay against the principle of your mortgage. Likewise, when people in your organization buy through Quixtar, a percentage is trapped in their business AND your business. The bigger the volume, the more money that's trapped and the more your business is worth.

> **Just as the government incentifies people to buy a home by offering interest deductions on income tax, Uncle Sam incentifies you to own your own business by offering tons of tax advantages.**

Home Ownership Principle #2: *Investments in your home can pay huge dividends.* Homeowners can increase the value of their home by *investing* time and money in painting, remodeling, landscaping, and so on. Likewise, by investing in books, tapes, tools, and live events that nurture personal growth and impart knowledge and know-how, IBOs can dramatically increase the value of "You, Inc," and, in doing so, can increase the volume and value of their Quixtar business.

Home Ownership Principle #3: *You can deduct the mortgage interest.* Just as the government incentifies people to buy a home by offering interest deductions on income tax, Uncle Sam incentifies you to own your own business by offering tons of tax advantages. As long as you keep good, accurate records, you can deduct your home office, travel, car expenses, food and lodging at live events, phone calls, and so on. In fact, business ownership is BY FAR the best tax-saving strategy available to the masses. Nothing else is even close.

So, there you have it—the perfect parallel between home ownership and business ownership. And the best part is, because you intuitively understand how to maximize building the value in your home, you don't have to learn a new skill or adopt a whole new way of thinking. All you have to do is apply the principles of homeownership to your Quixtar business, and then teach others to do the same.

Consumer Discounts vs. Business Discounts

*Men go shopping just as men go fishing—
to see how large a fish may be caught
with the smallest hook.*

—Henry Ward Beecher
minister

Now that you understand the perfect parallel between owning your own home and owning your Quixtar business, it's time to explore the difference between consumer discounts and business discounts. Let's start by looking at another homeowner scenario.

Joe and Mary just paid $150,000 for a home in a neighborhood surrounded by $300,000 homes. How did they get it so cheap? Because they followed a proven homeowner strategy—they bought the worst house in the best neighborhood with the idea of remodeling it themselves. They calculate that by investing in $50,000 worth of materials and "donating" their own labor, they can double the home's value by the end of the year, a forced savings of $100,000 ($300,000 minus $150,000 for the purchase price plus $50,000 of improvements).

Joe and Mary are very "smart" shoppers. They comb the papers looking for discounts on their remodeling materials. They buy tile at 50% discount. They buy hardwood for 10 cents on the dollar at an inventory closeout sale. They paint the inside and outside themselves. For one year they live in one bedroom and use one bathroom while the rest of the house is totally remodeled. At the end of the year, their house is a showcase! As a result, they've raised the value of their home to $300,000.

Business discounts get trapped... while consumer discounts disappear down a trap door!

But because Joe and Mary are smart shoppers and hard workers, they finish the renovation for only $30,000, instead of the $50,000 they had budgeted, a savings of $20,000. When it comes time to sell the house, do they lower the sales price $20,000? Not a chance! They'd sell for the full market price and put the extra $20,000 in their pockets, wouldn't they? When smart business owners receive business discounts, *they don't lower their sales price. They increase their profits!* The $20,000 Joe and Mary saved buying materials at discount is a *business discount because the money they saved is trapped in their home.*

Okay, now let's look at *consumer discounts.* Joe and Mary were able to trap a lot of money in their home through smart business discounts, but, unfortunately, they don't understand the difference between business discounts and consumer discounts. So, when it's time to buy consumable products for the home, they make a bee-line to this-mart and that-mart and buy everything on sale. They clip coupons for household products and they drive 100 miles on weekends to a giant outlet mall for their clothes. By the end of the year, they've bought $20,000 worth of stuff on sale for only $10,000, furnishing their home and stocking the pantries. And they tell their friends that by buying everything at 50% discount, they've "saved" $10,000.

But wait—where is the $10,000 they say they've "saved" by shopping for consumer discounts? Is it trapped in the home, like the business discounts? No. It's nowhere to be found! Therein lies the difference between business discounts and consumer discounts. Business discounts *get trapped...* while consumer discounts *disappear down a trap door!*

The Bigger the Volume, the Bigger the Business Discount

The easiest way for businesses to get discounts is to do lots of volume. In the restaurant business, for example, many of the restaurants in your city buy their steaks from the same supplier. But when the meat distributor gets an order from one local family restaurant, it might be for 100 filets per week. If that same distributor sells to the Outback Steakhouse chain of restaurants, the order might be for 10,000 filets per week shipped to 1,000 restaurants around the country. If the local family restaurant pays $6 per steak, Outback might pay $3.

> **The easiest way for businesses to get discounts is to do lots of volume.**

Let's say both Outback and the local family steakhouse charge the customer the same price for that steak, $12. The variable cost to the family steakhouse is $6, leaving a contribution margin of $6, correct? The variable cost to Outback is $3, leaving a contribution margin of $9, which is 50% higher than the family restaurant. Because business discounts are based on volume, Outback has an extra $3 trapped in their business.

So, I ask you, what does Outback do with the extra $3 that they just earned on volume discounts? Do they lower their menu prices for steak $3? Or do they keep the $3 in their business to contribute to their profit? Duh! *They keep it, of course!*

> **Your job isn't to quibble over the prices. Your job is to build volume so that your business discount reaches the highest level!**

Outback earned a big business discount by creating massive volume, didn't they? Consumer-think would tell them to lower their prices (and lower their profits in the process). But business-think told them that instead of lowering prices, it would be smarter to *increase the value of the customer's dining experience* while keeping their prices the same (thereby increasing their profits).

And that's exactly what they did—they trapped their volume discounts in their business and kept them there! As a result, Outback is the most profitable sit-down restaurant chain in the country. In fact, Outback is so profitable that Warren Buffett, arguably the most successful stock market investor in history, just added a ton of Outback Steakhouse stock to his $100-billion-plus portfolio. If that's not a ringing endorsement of Outback's business model, I don't know what is.

Be Like Outback—And Keep Your Profits In-House

The Quixtar Business Model is identical to the Outback business model in that the more volume you create, the deeper the business discounts you receive. And, like Outback, smart IBOs will seek to increase the value of their products and service, rather than discount the price of their products.

Look, when you have a product line like Quixtar's backed by world-class service and money-back guarantees, there's no need to lower prices. *The Quixtar price is right!* Your job isn't to quibble over the prices. Your job is to build volume so that your business discount reaches the highest level! You earn more money by building your volume, just as Outback does. Outback doesn't feel guilty about earning the biggest business discounts in their sector. They're thrilled! In fact, they're working hard to grow their business so they can get even bigger volume discounts and earn even bigger profits!

> **Quixtar Corporate offers business discounts from 3% to 25% in order to incentify IBOs to build more volume. So, why settle for a 3% business discount... or even an 18% business discount... when the company WANTS you to earn a 25% business discount?**

You should be the same way! Quixtar Corporate offers business discounts from 3% to 25% in order to incentify IBOs to build more volume. So, why settle for a 3% business discount... or even an 18% business discount... when the company WANTS you to earn a 25% business discount? Hello-o-o!

That's the big difference between consumer-think and business owner-think—consumers think of ways to spend less money to buy more stuff, and business owners think of ways to create more volume so they can make more money.

Let's see, which approach is geared to helping you live your dreams—spend less money by shopping for consumer discounts? Or make more money by building volume and trapping big business discounts?

All I know is this—every year in January, while most Americans are scurrying around shopping at post-Christmas sales, hundreds of Quixtar Diamonds are enjoying an all-expense-paid vacation in Hawaii, courtesy of Quixtar Corporate. Which means that during the coldest month of the year, *consumer discounts* will reserve you a place in the checkout line at Wal-Mart, while *business discounts* will reserve you a chaise longue on a beach in Hawaii to check out the sunset.

Which reservation do you prefer?

Aloha!

Pro-sumer Plus

Keep thy shop, and thy shop will keep thee.

—old English proverb

Having your dreams fulfilled is far more therapeutic than having them analyzed.

—Hyatt Resort advertisement

The late Lord Kenneth Thomson, a powerful newspaper magnate in Canada and one of the world's richest men, was a notorious cheapskate. How cheap was he? Despite owning dozens of businesses worth hundreds of millions, Thomson refused to have his picture taken so that he would go unrecognized when he shopped for socks on sale at the department store across the street from his office—and he *owned* the department store! *Now, that's cheap!*

(Thomson may have been laughingly cheap, but at least he got one thing right—he shopped at his own store! As I've always said, "Why buy from someone else at Their-Mart when you can buy from yourself at My-Mart?")

79

Remember When Service Was More Important Than Cost?

Psychiatrists would likely diagnose Thomson's passion for discounts as obsessive. But today, even "normal" people are obsessing over discounts. It wasn't that long ago that only poor people shopped at deep-discount stores. When I was growing up in the '50s and '60s, if you were middle class or above, you shopped at department stores. You wouldn't be caught dead in a discount store. Today, however, there are as many new fancy foreign cars and SUV's in the Wal-Mart parking lot as there are old junkers.

> **Today, even "normal" people are obsessing over discounts. It wasn't that long ago that only poor people shopped at deep discount stores.**

It used to be that people valued good service more than low prices. As I mentioned earlier in the book, I can remember when gas stations were called "service stations"—and for good reason. When I was a kid, customers weren't allowed to even *touch* the gas pump. We'd sit in the car while the attendant pumped the gas, washed all the windows, checked the oil, and measured the pressure in the tires. Yes, people paid a bit more per gallon for the service, but they thought it was worth it. Today, however, you can't find a service station, even if you are handicapped and need one.

I don't know about you, but I miss the days when the most popular business slogan was "Service is our middle name." I miss the days when the customer was always right. I miss the days when you could get a shoeshine and a shave at the barbershop, even if you didn't get your hair cut. I miss the days when the salesman at the clothing store knew your name and phoned you when the new spring or fall suits arrived. I miss the days when the butcher at the corner store would serve you a fresh joke along with fresh cuts of meat. I miss the days when a bag boy would carry your groceries out to the car and load them into the trunk for you. I miss the days when milk and ice cream were delivered to your door.

The Message and the Model Changed

What happened to great service? What happened to knowledgeable salespeople? What happened to convince shoppers that it was "smarter" to lug your groceries out to the car during a summer cloudburst rather than to have a bag boy do it if it would "save" you 50 cents on a case of Coke?

What happened is that since the 1950s, the *message* and the *model* have changed, and, as a result, our values have changed, too. How did the message and the model change? Beginning in the 1950s, the predominant cultural messages to the American people and the business models that delivered our consumer goods and services underwent a tremendous paradigm shift. Let's take a moment to look at why the shift occurred and how the new message and model have changed consumers' values and buying habits:

> I don't know about you, but I miss the days when the most popular business slogan was "Service is our middle name."

The cultural messages that prevailed in the pre-1950s could be best described as "Character Counts." Typical character counts messages were sayings like, "Work comes before play..."; "Anything worth doing is worth doing well..."; and "Slow and steady wins the race."

People received their Character Counts messages primarily from family and friends. These time-tested, wisdom-laden messages were meant as signposts to help guide us into becoming productive, prosperous, self-sufficient adults. Our parents' motives for delivering these messages were based on their genuine love and concern for our happiness and well-being and were untainted by commercialism. These messages were from loved ones to loved ones, from the heart to the heart, and were delivered to help us avoid disaster and achieve success by traveling the high road on our journey through life.

> **The cultural messages that prevailed in the pre-1950s could be best described as "Character Counts."**

In the 1950s, the new technology of television took over our living rooms and took over the role of delivering cultural messages to our children. Whereas the motives behind the Character Counts messages were motivated by love and a genuine concern for our well-being, the messages from the TV were motivated by money. Whereas the motives behind our parents' messages were solely altruistic, the motives behind the advertisers' messages were solely commercial. Advertisers quickly learned that it was a lot easier to sell products by pandering to pleasure rather than appealing to character. Advertisers couldn't care less about our character development. But they cared deeply about tapping into our pleasure zones.

So, they built their ad campaigns around Pleasure Pleasing messages, such as "If it feels good, do it...;" "It will make you irresistible to women...;" "It will make you beautiful...;" "It will make you popular...;" and so on. Thus, with each commercial break, yet another Pleasure Pleasing message was broadcast into our living rooms to be absorbed unchallenged by our children.

Our Parents' Messages Never Had a Chance

Predictably, there was a clash between the "old" Character Counts messages and the "new" Pleasure Pleasing messages. For example, our parents warned us not to smoke (even if they smoked) because it was bad for our health. This was a heartfelt, sincere message aimed at making us happier, healthier citizens. TV advertisers, on the other hand, glamorized smoking and told us to smoke because it would give us pleasure. This was a deceptive, commercial message aimed at making owners and executives of the TV networks and tobacco companies insanely rich. But when you're an impressionable child, which message carries more weight—the one delivered by your aging "hopelessly old-fashioned" parents? Or the message delivered by young, smiling Madison Avenue models telling you that they can't resist men who smoke Marlboros and wear Old Spice after shave? Truth is, once we invited TV advertisers into our homes to deliver their slick, consumer-think messages, our parents' messages never had a chance.

> **Whereas the motives behind our parents' messages were solely altruistic, the motives behind the advertisers' messages were solely commercial.**

How Traditional American Values Got Turned Inside Out and Upside Down

As TV grew in popularity, the Character Counts messages were gradually replaced by the Pleasure Pleasing messages, and in the turbulent '60s and '70s, many of our most treasured American values got turned upside down: Out became in. Down became up. Loser became winner. Bad became good. Naughty became nice. Rebellion became mainstream. Us became me. And spend became save. To better understand the major culture shift that occurred in the middle of the 20th century, let's compare the list of values from the pre-'50s generations to the post-'50s generations:

Character Counts Values	*Pleasure Principle Values*
1) Make more than you spend	Spend more than you make
2) Save now, buy later	Buy now, pay later
3) Work comes before play	Play now, for tomorrow may never come
4) Self-reliance	Entitlement
5) There's no free lunch	The world owes me a living
6) Slow and steady	Get rich quick
7) Delayed gratification	Instant gratification
8) Self-made man	He got his, where's mine?
9) Self-discipline	Do your own thing
10) Save by putting money aside	"Save" by buying stuff on sale

Now, what does all of this have to do with discounts and pricing? Simply this: With the introduction of TV, advertisers began a devious campaign to increase sales by aggressively manipulating consumers into believing that "saving" money and spending money were really the same thing. Here's what happened:

Not only did manufacturers and stores make it much easier to buy, they also began encouraging us to spend a bigger and bigger percentage of our hard-earned dollars in their store. More and more stores started using the word "save" as a synonym for "spend" in their advertising, with headlines like, "Big Savings." "Save more." "Savings up to 70% off!" "Save on everyday low prices." " Buy direct... and save!" "A savings of $100 when you buy two." Marketing research shows that the two words that have the most dramatic, measurable impact on sales are "save" and "free," which, of course, culminated in the ultimate marketing slogan, "Get one free... and save!"

In other words, because TV re-programmed us and changed our character-thinking to consumer-thinking, most Americans really and truly believe that they can "save" by buying at discount. As a result, today Americans own a lot of worthless gadgets they don't need and seldom use, but they have little or no money in savings or investments, outside the equity in their home. So sad. So unnecessary. And *so avoidable!*

> **As TV grew in popularity, the Character Counts messages were gradually replaced by the Pleasure Pleasing messages, and in the turbulent '60s and '70s, many of our most treasured American values got turned upside down.**

How the Message Has Shaped the Model

The Pleasure Pleasing message that people can "save" by buying at discount changed not only consumers themselves, but also the business models that distributed goods and services to discount-desperate consumers. More and more demand for discounts naturally led to more and more discount stores. Since the definition of price is "what you have to give up to get what you want," the discount stores had to give up friendly service and nice environments in exchange for charging less for their products.

For example, when I was in high school, I used to visit the local ACE Hardware store. The front half of the store was for customers. The storefront had clean linoleum floors, shoulder-high shelves, recessed lights, and spotless counters. If the owner couldn't find what I wanted on the shelves, he'd disappear into the warehouse through a door marked, EMPLOYEES ONLY! In contrast to storefront, the warehouse had cement floors, ceiling-high shelves packed with dusty, half-empty boxes, exposed plumbing and electrical service, and unpainted, cinder-block walls. The nice part of the store was reserved for customers. Because the warehouse was raw and unfinished, it was off limits to everyone but employees.

> **With the introduction of TV, advertisers began a devious campaign to increase sales by aggressively manipulating consumers into believing that "saving" money and spending money were really the same thing.**

But as the demand for discounts grew, the hardware industry responded by eliminating the storefront and transposing the warehouse from a backroom operation into a full-scale business model. The Home Depot was born. Instead of hiding the warehouse in the back, The Home Depot promoted the warehouse to the front, which attracted even more consumers, who had convinced themselves that the best stuff and the lowest prices were in the warehouse anyway.

The more consumers demand to "save" by buying at discounts, the more the business models respond by building bigger, uglier stores and hiring skeleton crews of minimum-wage clerks who don't know the product line, don't like working, and don't care if your needs are being met or not (with the singular exception of The Home Depot, who, I must admit, do a great job of staffing their stores with plenty of knowledge-able, helpful clerks). Instead of employees acting as if "the customer is always right," today employees act as if the customer is a nuisance who must be ignored or avoided until the next cigarette break. Yep, over the last 50 years, the message and the model have changed from "service with a smile"... to self-serve with a frown.

Welcome to the Age of the Deep Discount!

Opportunity Knocks

Today, the obsessive demand for discounts has forced many companies to change their business models. More and more the trend is moving away from "Service is our middle name" to "Everyday low prices." As a result, discount mania has transformed shopping from an activity that people used to enjoy to a chore that they try to avoid at all costs.

Hark! That pounding sound you hear is opportunity knocking!

You see, the demand for discounts is really a blessing in disguise. People are tired of dealing with surly, unsmiling clerks who don't know where anything is or how much it costs. People are tired of crowded parking lots and sloth-slow checkout lanes. People are tired of returning items and being told that "All sales are final" or "We can only give you credit, not cash, because you forgot your receipt." People are tired of asking a clerk which product they should buy only to hear, "I dunno. I just work here." In other words, people are tired of the "new" message and model. People are desperate to return to the days when the one-and-only message was Character Counts, and the dominant business models were based primarily on quality and service.

> **Over the last 50 years, the message and the model have changed from "Service with a smile"... to self-serve with a frown.**

But wait!—that galloping sound you hear is Quixtar to the rescue!

Quixtar is perfectly positioned to rescue frustrated, stressed-out shoppers from the downside of Discount Mania. I'm convinced that today, more than any time in the last 50 years, shoppers are open to alternative shopping experiences that save them time, effort, and stress, while offering quality products at fair and reasonable prices. And I'm also convinced that because of a stagnant global economy and because of corporate America's penchant for laying off workers and eliminating pensions, today more and more people are open to exploring the opportunity of business ownership. Now let's take a look at how Quixtar offers two high-demand opportunities in one business model—a *shopping opportunity* for weary consumers; and a *business opportunity* for dissatisfied employees and disillusioned traditional business owners. Let's start by briefly discussing the shopping opportunity associated with Quixtar.

The Quixtar Shopping Opportunity and Consumer Discounts

In the last chapter we discussed the difference between consumer discounts and business discounts. You learned that although *consumer discounts* don't really "save" people money, they do allow people to buy more stuff for less money. *Business discounts,* on the other hand, make people money because the savings are trapped in the business.

If you're talking to people about the Quixtar *shopping opportunity,* then you'll want to explain the great consumer discounts available through Quixtar because consumers want to know how to stretch their dollars by buying more stuff for less money. On the other hand, if you're talking to people about the Quixtar *business opportunity,* you'll want to concentrate on the business discounts, because business people want to know how the money is made.

> **People are desperate to return to the days when the one-and-only message was Character Counts, and the dominant business models were based primarily on quality and service.**

Let's start by talking about the consumer discounts available through the Quixtar shopping opportunity. Let me begin our discussion by saying that during my travels around the country and the world giving speeches to Quixtar audiences, I've talked with hundreds of new IBOs and eager prospects. And invariably during one of these conversations, someone will tell me that they wished Quixtar were a discount buying club so that "everyone would want to join."

I've heard this comment enough times that I decided it was time to do some research. Rather than assume that the prices at discount stores were lower than Quixtar's prices, I decided to visit the local Publix, a major supermarket chain that constantly advertises low sale prices in order to compare their prices to three of Quixtar's flagship products— SA8 detergent, L.O.C. multi-purpose cleaner, and Nutrilite supplements.

Factoring in concentration, SA8 and L.O.C. were pennies apart from their name-brand counterparts. Factoring in quality, efficiency, and environmental friendliness, the Quixtar line was a far better value.

The first challenge I had was to find leading-brand products that were comparable in quality to Quixtar's products. Sure, Publix had dozens of laundry detergents, household cleaners, and vitamins. But I couldn't find a single brand-name detergent that was concentrated *and* biodegradable. As for household cleaners, although several of the brand-name cleaners were concentrated, none was biodegradable. As far as the Nutrilite line is concerned, Double X has up to 16 times the vitamin levels and 7 times the mineral levels as leading-brand Centrum. Which means that instead of comparing prices of "apples to apples," I ended up comparing the prices of Centrum's crab apples to Quixtar's Red Delicious apples.

Despite the disparity in quality and environmental friendliness, I discovered that the cost of SA8 and L.O.C. at the member discount level compared favorably to all of the leading brands in their categories. Factoring in concentration, SA8 and L.O.C. were pennies apart from their name-brand counterparts. Factoring in quality, efficiency, and environmental friendliness, the Quixtar line was a far better value. The cost of the Nutrilite line was higher than Centrum, but given the fact that someone would have to take five to 16 times more Centrum to get the same amount of vitamins and minerals as Double X, the added cost of Double X was more than justified.

> **"Quixtar is a QUALITY discount store that delivers to your door. They shouldn't be copying Wal-Mart's business model. Wal-Mart should be copying theirs!"**

In conclusion, when you compare discount price to discount price... product to product... quality to quality... Quixtar products are comparable in price and value to any product in the marketplace. That's why I say the Quixtar price is right—that's just a fact! But it's the intangibles that puts the real shine on the Quixtar shopping opportunity. Considering that "price is what you have to give up to get what you want," just consider all of the *intangibles that are added to the Quixtar shopping opportunity.* No traffic jams. No long checkout lines. No unmotivated, minimum-wage clerks. Quixtar offers hassle-free ordering via the phone or the Internet. Delivery to your door. Iron-clad, 100% money-back guarantees. And customized, automatic replenishment backed by a content-rich secure website loaded with thousands of pages of product information and needs analysis. It doesn't get any better than that.

In the future when people comment to me that "Quixtar should become a discount store so that everyone would want to join," I'm going to reply, "Quixtar is a *quality* discount store that delivers to your door. They shouldn't be copying Wal-Mart's business model. Wal-Mart should be copying theirs!"

> Never lose sight of the fact that the Quixtar shopping opportunity is for consumers, while the Quixtar business opportunity is for pro-sumers. The best that discount-driven consumers can hope for is to get poorer slower. The best dedicated pro-sumers can hope for is to grow richer quicker.

Know When to Speak Consumer-Think

Okay, we just established that when quality and concentration are factored in, Quixtar products compare favorably in price to any brand, anywhere. But unfortunately, some consumers are so conditioned by consumer-think that they're unable to think outside the "buying-smarter-means-buying-cheaper" box. In other words, no matter how compelling the evidence, some discount addicts can't hear your words because they're deaf to any messages other than, "Smart shoppers buy at discount and save!" In this case, follow the old axiom, "When in Rome, do as the Romans do." If discounts and deals are all a person can comprehend, then tell them what they want to hear by pointing out the great discounts and deals available through Quixtar!

Explain how shoppers can qualify for immediate discounts by becoming Quixtar Members, PLUS show them how to access the "Hot Buys" section on Quixtar.com.

Discount addicts will LOVE the Features/Specials section and will positively drool over the items featured in the Clearance Store. In addition, many of the Partner Stores feature regular discounts, such as "Discount Movies and Music" and "Discounted Wireless and Cell Phones." If special discounts and great deals aren't enough, then steer your discount-driven friends to the Quixtar auction site, where consumers can set their own prices for selected items from participating partner stores.

> **No one ever got rich shopping at discount, but many, MANY people have gotten rich by offering high-demand products and services at fair and reasonable prices.**

If a prospect can't get past consumer-think, that's their decision. But don't allow their discount dependency to rob you of your dreams. Never lose sight of the fact that the Quixtar *shopping opportunity is for consumers,* while the Quixtar *business opportunity is for pro-sumers.* The best that discount-driven consumers can hope for is to get poorer slower. The best dedicated pro-sumers can hope for is to grow richer quicker.

The Quixtar Business Opportunity and Business Discounts

Yes, the Quixtar shopping opportunity offers consumer discounts that are just as generous as any Big-Mart and Cost-Less Warehouse in existence. And, yes, there's nothing wrong with discussing discounts with people who are locked into consumer-think. But when you're talking discounts with people, keep in mind that discounts may fill the temporary need of some robot consumers. But always remember the first rule of business-ownership: *No one ever got rich shopping at discount, but many, MANY people have gotten rich by offering high-demand products and services at fair and reasonable prices.*

Quixtar products are priced to sell, which is good news for consumers; and priced for profit, which is great news for business owners. And as a business owner, you should be more concerned about increasing profits than lowering prices.

For example, I don't think I've ever bought a single Microsoft product on sale. When I bought Microsoft Office two years ago, I paid full retail. I didn't bother shopping around because I knew the price would be about the same, whether I got it at Costco or Best Buy or off the Internet. Yet, despite the fact that most consumers are discount crazy, Bill Gates continues to sell his products for full retail. The result? Gates is the richest man in the world. He couldn't care less about consumer discounts. But rest assured, he's VERY concerned about business discounts, because that's where the profits come from. Case closed.

The Business Opportunity and Business Discounts

Okay, we've established that Quixtar's one-of-a-kind products, along with the concentrated, biodegradable formulas and great consumer discounts plus the many intangibles, make the Quixtar shopping opportunity clearly superior to the discount model. Indeed, from a consumer standpoint, Quixtar is in a class by itself.

Now it's time to look at the business opportunity in light of the business discounts. You'll be delighted to know that the Quixtar price is right not only for consumers, but also for business owners. What I mean is that the Quixtar products are *priced to sell,* which is good news for consumers; and *priced for profit,* which is great news for business owners. And as a business owner, you should be more concerned about increasing profits than lowering prices. Lower prices is consumer-think, and, as we just established, Quixtar prices are fair and reasonable and often less expensive than comparable products sold through discount retail stores.

As a business person, it's your job to move potential business owners away from consumer-think to business owner-think. Once you decide to work the business, you need to put your consumer-think on ice and concentrate on learning how to trap more money in your business by increasing the number and degree of your business discounts. And the only way to do that is to increase your business volume.

> **To increase your profits, you have to increase your volume. And it's far easier to increase your volume by opening multiple stores across the country and around the world than by focusing on building one huge store in only one location.**

From Pro-sumer to Pro-sumer Plus

In my book, *Pro-sumer Power!*, I made this statement: *"If you want to have more, think like a store."* What I mean is that people who are serious about time and money freedom need to think like the owner of a store—the one *making the money*—as opposed to the shoppers in the store—the ones *spending the money*.

If your goal is to grow your wealth, you have to grow your business, right? And there are basically two ways to grow a business. You can increase your volume by expanding one small store until it becomes one GIANT store, thereby increasing your profits by selling more stuff at bigger business discounts (the more stuff you buy, the bigger the business discount you receive).

> **To maximize the Quixtar opportunity, you need to think like a chain, for you can create 1,000 times the volume in the chain concept than you can in the single-store concept. That's why I say, "For maximum gain, think like a chain."**

A perfect example of growing your business by building a giant store is The Tattered Cover book store in Denver, Colorado. Over the last 25 years, the original store was expanded three times until it has become the largest bookstore in the country. Today The Tattered Cover houses nearly half a million books on four floors, along with a coffee shop and a fourth-floor restaurant. There's no question that The Tattered Cover is a success story and has made the owner a very wealthy person.

But the one-giant-store concept has limitations. No matter how big you grow one store, you can only serve a limited number of customers because *a single store is limited to serving a single region*. Over the years business owners have overcome the limitations of the one-giant-store business model by opening numerous stores across the country. For example, instead of building one or two giant regional bookstores, Barnes & Noble decided to open hundreds of chain stores across the country. The biggest Barnes & Noble store is much smaller than The Tattered Cover, but Barnes & Noble does TONS more volume than The Tattered Cover because the chain stores enable them to reach millions more people in hundreds more regions of the country.

The same principle applies to your Quixtar business. To increase your profits, you have to increase your volume. And it's far easier to increase your volume by opening multiple stores across the country and around the world than by focusing on building one huge store in only one location. In other words, the essence of pro-suming is, "If you want to have more, think like a store." But to maximize the Quixtar opportunity, you need to think like a chain, for you can create 1,000 times the volume in the chain concept than you can in the single store concept. That's why I say, *"For maximum gain, think like a chain."* For when you think and act like a chain, you begin to move from a pro-sumer... to a pro-sumer plus!

> **The Quixtar business model was designed to avoid the pain that faces every chain— huge variable and fixed costs. The cost of entry for Quixtar IBOs is ridiculously small, especially in light of the upside potential.**

And when you become a pro-sumer plus, the jet engines of the Quixtar business opportunity really start to kick into high gear!

Personal Franchising: Gain Like a Chain... Without the Pain

For sure, thinking and acting like a chain is necessary to growing your business. But increased revenues doesn't necessarily guarantee increased profits. Kmart, for example, takes in more revenues today than they did 10 years ago. But 10 years ago they were showing a profit, whereas today they're losing money hand over fist. How can they be taking in more money but earning less? Expenses. Yes, gross revenues at Kmart increased during the '90s. But expenses increased at an even greater rate than revenues, resulting in losses, quarter after quarter.

> **The Quixtar business model takes the best of the chain concept—and leaves the rest. In other words, Quixtar IBOs can gain like a chain without the pain! How can they do that? By performing more like a personal franchise than a chain.**

That's one of the downsides to the chain-store business model—the expenses are enormous! In order for chains to expand, they have to order more inventory. Build more stores. Hire more people. Take out more loans. And, at the end of the quarter, all too often the total of the expenses is greater than the total of the revenues. (When expenses exceed revenues, you either right the ship quickly... or you write the ship off, because companies that don't make profits don't last very long.)

The Quixtar business model was designed to avoid the pain that faces every chain—huge variable and fixed costs. The cost of entry for Quixtar IBOs is ridiculously small, especially in light of the upside potential. And, as we learned in Chapter 5, the variable costs and fixed costs associated with being a Quixtar IBO are not only minimal, they can REMAIN minimal, even when your gross revenues continue to grow by leaps and bounds.

By their very nature, chain stores must incur HUGE expenses in order to even hope to generate more revenues. The cash outlay and the financial risk to chains is frightening. But the Quixtar business model takes the best of the chain concept—and leaves the rest. In other words, *Quixtar IBOs can gain like a chain without the pain!* How can they do that? By performing more like a *personal franchise* than a chain.

If you want to have more, Think like a store. For maximum gain, Think like a chain. But to be truly wise, Think personal franchise!

You see, the franchising concept was an ingenious improvement on the chain business model for the simple reason that the franchise concept *encourages expansion and growth but at a fraction of the cost.* The Quixtar personal franchise model takes the franchise concept to a whole new level! Why do I say that? Because the upfront investment and the on-going fixed and variable costs to run a profitable Quixtar business are absurdly low. Territories are unrestricted (80 countries, and counting). The business grows exponentially, not linearly, like traditional franchises. No employees are needed. And last but not least, successful business partners want you to surpass their level of success.

No other business model has these features PLUS the added advantage of being able to launch your business by working part-time in the evenings and weekends while keeping your full-time job. You certainly can't say that about the chain concept. Or the franchise concept, for that matter.

But the personal franchise offers you all of these advantages, along with a virtually unlimited income potential. Now are you beginning to see where the "plus" in pro-sumer plus comes from? The best way to sum up the advantages of pro-sumer plus is to end with a rhyme (with sincere apologies to James Thurber).

If you want to have more,

Think like a store.

For maximum gain,

Think like a chain.

But to be truly wise,

Think personal franchise!

The Purpose of Business

*In the end, it is impossible to have a great
life unless it is a meaningful life. And it's
very difficult to have a meaningful life
without meaningful work.*

—Jim Collins
"Good to Great"

When Buddy Post, a former carnival worker, won $16.2 million in the Pennsylvania lottery in 1988, he thought all of his troubles were over.

Think again, Buddy!

In the months immediately following his winning jackpot, Post was convicted of assault... his sixth wife left him... his brother tried to kill him... and his landlady successfully sued him for one-third of his winnings. If this is what happens when the guy has good luck, I'd hate to see what his bad luck looks like!

What lesson can we learn from the Buddy Post saga? Well, for one thing it reminds us that money can't buy happiness. We all know people with money who are miserable. If someone is an emotional mess when they're broke, they'll likely be an emotional mess when they become rich—and, more than likely, they'll burn through their newfound fortune trying to buy happiness in all the wrong places.

Motives, not Money, Cause Misery

I think a lot of people enjoy hearing riches-to-rags stories because it confirms their misconception that money is the root of all evil. That's why you hear people say things like, "I don't want a lot of money because I don't want to become materialistic." Or, "Rich people are stuck up, and I don't want to forget my roots." Or, "The bigger your bank account, the bigger your problems." Or, "The best things in life are free, so I don't really care if I have more money or not." Or, "Money just makes you greedy for more money, so you're never really happy." Or, "I don't want to make money on my friends."

> **Look, the truth is that money doesn't lead irrevocably to materialism any more than poverty leads irrevocably to crime.**

It used to make me angry when I'd hear comments like this, because I know that people who say these things are just rationalizing their anemic net worth. But instead of getting angry, now I get sad, because it makes me sad to see so many people with so much potential give up on themselves and their dreams.

Look, the truth is that money doesn't lead irrevocably to materialism any more than poverty leads irrevocably to crime. I know many, many wealthy people who are humble and non-materialistic, and just as happy as they can be. Money doesn't cause misery. In fact, money can alleviate misery if it's used in the right way. Let's face it, churches and children's hospitals don't build themselves. Churches and non-profit hospitals are built by donated dollars. And if you talk with any pastor or president of a non-profit organization, they'll tell you that 80% to 90% of their building funds come from a handful of people.

For example, a friend of mine attends a Methodist church in Tampa. The church just recently built a spectacular $3.2-million sanctuary to accommodate its 900-family congregation. If the costs were borne equally, each family would have contributed about $3,500 to the building fund. But what happened was that 12 families contributed $2.9 million to the campaign. Another 80 givers contributed an additional $200,000. And another hundred or so families contributed a total of $50,000, leaving the campaign $50,000 short of its $3.2-million goal. So, how much did the remaining 700 families donate to the building fund? Zero. Not one red cent.

> **Money doesn't cause misery. In fact, money can alleviate misery if it's used in the right way. Let's face it, churches and children's hospitals don't build themselves. Churches and non-profit hospitals are built by donated dollars.**

So much for the theory that money corrupts people and makes them greedy. In fact, evidence shows that the opposite is true—it's not money but the LACK OF MONEY that makes people needy and greedy. Truth is, if more people had more money, there would be a lot more happy, fulfilled, generous people in this world, that's for sure. It's not money that causes misery. It's *motives* that cause misery. If someone is a self-centered jerk when they're poor, they'll just be bigger self-centered jerk when they're rich. But if someone is kind and temperate and giving when they're poor, they'll just be more of the same when they're rich. Money doesn't corrupt people. Money is just a magical magnifying glass that enlarges people's character and super-sizes their values.

The Difference between Greed and Need

It always amazes me that so many people in this country are anti-business. I deal with this anti-business sentiment every day from some of my teaching associates at the university.

It's not money that causes misery. It's motives that cause misery.

You should have seen how some of my left-leaning colleagues lit up when the Enron scandal became headline news. They were in hog heaven. They railed against big business. They railed against President Bush's proposed tax cut. They railed against government deregulation policies. But when I pointed out that the university system is supported by taxes and tuition, and the more money that corporations earn, the more salary college teachers can earn, the lefties change the subject.

But the scandals at Enron and Tyco do bring up two challenging questions:

1) What's the difference between need and greed?

2) Is there any purpose in business other than making a profit?

Let's start by answering the first question, "What's the difference between need and greed?" Webster's defines greed as "the excessive desire for wealth; desire for more than one needs or deserves." Now, I seldom disagree with Mr. Webster, but he missed the boat on this one. I don't think greed is a matter of desire or deserving. I think it's more a matter of ethics.

For example, Bill Gates and Warren Buffett are good buddies and the two richest men in the world. They didn't earn hundreds of billions EACH because they lacked desire for money. These guys are businessmen! Their goal is to make money. The more, the merrier. Are they driven and successful? Yes. Are they greedy? No. Why? Because they provide valuable products and services to people at a fair and reasonable price while conducting their businesses ethically and with integrity. That's not to say both guys are perfect. They've both made mistakes because they're such aggressive businessmen. But unethical and unscrupulous? Not in my book.

> **Money doesn't corrupt people. Money is just a magical magnifying glass that enlarges people's character and super-sizes their values.**

Now, compare Gates and Buffett to Dennis Kozlowski, former CEO of Tyco. Kozlowski was indicted on charges of looting Tyco of hundreds of millions through improper loans to himself and 41 other Tyco employees. He also illegally spent another $100 million or so on homes for himself and top employees and tens of millions more on personal expenditures purchased with company money, including $15,000 for an umbrella stand, $6,400 for a shower curtain, and $97,000 for fresh-cut flowers for his $2.5-million Trump Tower apartment in Manhattan. The plundering CEO didn't stop there. Under Kozlowski's direction, Tyco avoided paying tens of millions of dollars in tax dollars by incorporating in Bermuda, even though Tyco made the lion's share of its profits from American consumers. In other words, Kozlowski was so sleazy that he was stealing money from Tyco while he was manipulating ways for Tyco to steal money from the government. Now, THAT'S GREEDY!

> **The purpose of business is twofold: to make a profit and to make a positive difference in people's lives.**

Like Gates and Buffett, Kozlowski has an "excessive desire for wealth." But what makes Kozlowski greedy isn't the degree of his desire, but his lack of honesty and integrity. The guy's a crook! He was greedy because he wanted money so badly that he stole, lied, maneuvered, cheated, connived, and forged to get it. He was greedy because he didn't care what he did or who he hurt in order to line his own pockets. I say, "Toss the jerk in jail and throw away the key!"

Making a Profit and Making a Difference

Okay, now we move on to the second question, "Is making a profit the only purpose of business?" Well, certainly making a profit is one purpose of business. That goes without saying. But it's not the only purpose. The way I see it, the purpose of business is twofold: *to make a profit and to make a positive difference in people's lives.*

Now, why would I say that making a positive difference in people's lives is just as important as making a profit? The best way to answer that question is to retell the story that Steven Covey uses in his best-selling book, *7 Habits of Highly Effective People.* Covey argues that success isn't just about how much money you make. Success is also tied to how *meaningful* your work is. To prove his point, he gives the example of a job that pays a million dollars a year. But the job requirement is to dig a hole the first half of the day, then spend the second half of the day filling it back in. But to earn the million dollars a year, you'd have to dig the hole and fill it back in every day, six days a week, for 40 years. Would you take the job?

Hey, I'd love to earn a million dollars a year, wouldn't you? But there's no way I would perform a meaningless task eight hours a day... six days a week... day in and day out... year in and year out... from the time I was 25 until I was 65, for any amount of money. No way. What about you?

How You Earn Money Is More Important Than How Much You Earn

Look, I know that money isn't everything in life. But it's a BIG thing, and we might as well recognize that money has the power to do a lot more good than bad for ourselves, for our families, and for our communities.

But I'd be the first to admit that HOW you earn your money is MORE important than HOW MUCH you earn. For example, there are thousands of drug lords around the world who make A LOT more money than even the highest-earning Quixtar IBO. From what I've read in the newspapers, the big drug kingpins run their illegal trades in the same manner as CEOs of reputable businesses. They choose a board of directors. They set up departments and coordinate marketing and distribution functions. They control expenses to maximize profits. They invest money back into their business. They

> **HOW you earn your money is MORE important than HOW MUCH you earn.**

plan strategies and draw up action plans. In short, many drug lords run their illegal enterprises as businesses and, as a result, earn enormous profits. But are they making a positive difference in people's lives? *Of course not!* Their products and their "management teams" destroy lives and terrorize communities, which proves that when all is said and done, making a difference is often MORE important than making a profit.

Trained to Believe That Making a Profit and Making a Difference Were Incompatible

I must admit that I didn't always believe someone could make a profit and make a positive difference at the same time. Back in the '60s and '70s when I was attending high school and college, I believed that making a profit and making a difference were polar opposites and that you had to choose one or the other. Like a lot of young people in those decades, I bought into some silly, oversimplified myths about business, money, and social class. For example, I thought rich people got rich by exploiting poor people. Therefore, I reasoned, rich people were bad and poor people were good. I thought that rich people lived phony, plastic lives, as opposed to poor people, whose lives were genuine and authentic. I downplayed the importance of money and convinced myself that poverty was ennobling. I reasoned that because only mean, selfish people chose to make money, and, because I was good and giving, I would opt to forgo making money in favor of making a difference in people's lives.

> **To make a difference in people's lives, you have to make a difference in your own life first.**

So, at age 21, armed with optimism and idealism, I joined VISTA (an acronym for Volunteer In Service To America), the domestic version of the Peace Corps. In 1974, I was sent to Cleveland and assigned living quarters in an inner city housing project where 95% of the tenants were on welfare. My job was to help minorities start businesses, which is a noble cause if there ever was one. I was paid $100 a week.

> **Wealth-draining social systems are set up to reward poverty, whereas wealth-creating business systems are set up to reward productivity.**

I went to Cleveland as a liberal 21-year-old determined to serve as a soldier in the war on poverty. When I left Cleveland a year later, I was a conservative 22-year-old determined to spend my remaining years driving as much distance between myself and poverty as humanly possibly.

A Teacher Learns His Lessons

You see, I went to Cleveland to save the world. But I ended up saving myself. I went to Cleveland to teach poor people how to break the cycle of poverty. But I ended up teaching myself some hard-won lessons about the meanness inherent in our failed liberal social programs.

Here's what I learned in Cleveland:

I learned that if you want to make a difference in people's lives, you have to make a difference in your own life first.

I learned that there was no dignity in poverty, only desperation.

I learned that most poor people were poor for a reason—they didn't work.

I learned that when the government GIVES people food and shelter for free, it TAKES AWAY the incentive to work and pride of accomplishment.

I learned that the job of social workers wasn't to get people out of poverty but to help people get really good at remaining poor.

There's no government big enough or rich enough to save people from themselves.

I learned that the ideas that didn't work revolved around getting something for nothing, whereas the ideas that did work revolved around getting paid for a valuable service or product.

I learned that wealth-draining social systems are set up to reward poverty, whereas wealth-creating business systems are set up to reward productivity.

I learned that there's no government big enough or rich enough to save people from themselves.

Most of all, I learned that making a positive difference in people's lives and making a profit go hand in hand.

That's what I learned during my one year in Cleveland—and the lessons I learned there will never, ever be forgotten.

Paying the Price for Success

My year in Cleveland was an eye-opener for me, that's for sure. It taught me that although there's no simple, one-size-fits-all solution to life's biggest challenges, conservatism's "Compassionate Capitalism" is far more helpful and productive for far more people than its liberal counterpart, "Liberal Love."

Today I make no apologies for wanting to make more money in my life while making a positive difference in other people's lives... and neither should you. Yes, most of this book was dedicated to teaching you how to make more profits in your business. But I do want to remind you that when you share the Quixtar opportunity, you are also in the enviable position to make a big, BIG difference in people's lives, including your own life. Very few people can make such a boast, and you should never take your mission lightly.

Although there's no simple, one-size-fits-all solution to life's biggest challenges, conservatism's "Compassionate Capitalism" is far more helpful and productive for far more people than its liberal counterpart, "Liberal Love."

When an interviewer asked Florine Mark, the founder of Weight Watchers, how she would describe her business, she replied, "We sell self-respect." As a Quixtar IBO, you sell self-respect, too. But you also sell self-empowerment and self-determination.

Never forget that you've chosen the Quixtar business model for a reason. Perhaps you're seeking to make more of a difference in people's lives. Or more money. Or more freedom. Or more control. Or more time with your family. Or more self-respect. These are all wonderful, worthwhile dreams, and you should nurture them and keep them safe.

Truth is, if you're focusing on the price of the products you're likely to lose sight of your dreams. You're better off concentrating on higher goals than lower prices. If you're determined to focus on price, then focus on the price you're willing to pay for time and money freedom.

Always remember—the Quixtar price is right.

But your dreams? They're priceless.